# DISCOVERY
## *IN THE* NORTH
## ATLANTIC

# DISCOVERY
## *IN THE* NORTH
# ATLANTIC

## *J.J. SHARP*

NIMBUS
PUBLISHING LTD

Nimbus Publishing Limited
P.O. Box 9301, Station A
Halifax, Nova Scotia
B3K 5N5

Cover illustration: [Ships and Whales in a Tempest].
Oil on panel, by Hendrik Cornelisz Vroom (c. 1610).
Courtesy Kendall Whaling Museum, Sharon, Massachusetts, U.S.A.

Cover design: Arthur Carter, Halifax
Printing and binding: Hignell Printing Limited, Winnipeg

Canadian Cataloguing in Publication Data

Sharp, J.J. (James Jack), 1939-
Discovery in the North Atlantic
ISBN 0-921054-89-0
1. Discoveries (in geography) 2. North Atlantic
Region—Discovery and exploration. I. Title.
G89.S52 1991 910'.9163'1 C91-097639-2

Printed and bound in Canada

# CONTENTS

# INTRODUCTION

When the three ships commanded by Christopher Columbus, the *Niña,* the *Pinta,* and the *Santa Maria,* sailed into sight of the West Indies in 1492, they changed the face of the world as it was then known. Columbus's voyage was the first of three major expeditions which opened up the globe for European expansion. Vasco da Gama's trip round the Cape of Good Hope and on to the East, as well as Ferdinand Magellan's exploration of the Pacific and his crew's circumnavigation of the world, took place within fifteen years of Columbus's first voyage. Spaniards and Portuguese rushed to take advantage of the new lands as the opportunities for wealth expanded. Within fifty years the Portuguese established their pre-eminence in the Indian Ocean and along the Malabar coast, while Spanish merchants and priests were eagerly subduing the southern parts of the New World. Other nations, coming later to the scene, were forced to look to northern latitudes for adventure, profit, and easy routes to the East.

European interest in the fabulous wealth of Cathay (China) and Cipangu (Japan) had been developing since the Venetian-born Marco Polo had recounted his travels to an astonished audience in the late thirteenth century. In 1256, Marco's father and uncle, Niccolo and Maffeo Polo, were on a trading mission in Constantinople. Before returning to Venice, they decided to cross the Black Sea, but due to an outbreak of war, they instead journeyed east through Bukhara, Samarkand, and Turkistan, finally crossing the entire Asian continent until they reached the court of the great Kublai Khan in Peking, where they stayed more than ten years before sailing for home.

On their next voyage, beginning in 1271, they took with them the seventeen-year-old Marco, who did not return to Venice for twenty-odd years. During all that time he kept journals describing his travels in the East. These were later transcribed while he was in prison, during the war between Venice and Genoa, three years after his return. When published, his detailed descriptions, despite their accuracy, were widely disbelieved by an incredulous public because no one could accept that such an advanced, wealthy and cultured civilization could be anything other then a figment of his imagination. Even today, it is difficult to comprehend how such a tremendously advanced city like Kinsai could have existed in the thirteenth century. To the medieval European mind it was unimaginable. A conservative estimate can be made of the population of Kinsai at that time, based on Marco's description of the guild system, which was remarkable in itself. The work of the city was organized into 12 main guilds, one for each craft, and every guild had about 12,000 workshops, each employing between 10 and 40 men. Therefore the workshop population, not including women and children, might have been around 3 million, and this was at a time when the total population of Portugal was less than 1,250,000. It is little wonder Marco's descriptions fell on deaf ears. Nevertheless, despite the incredulity which met the publication of his book, it was not long before others, particularly missionaries, made similar journeys and came back with similar accounts. As more and more information became available, trade routes gradually developed, bringing Eastern goods across Asia and through the Mediterranean to the bustling markets of Europe.

Between 1000 and 1350 AD, the population of Europe quadrupled and trade increased tremendously, perhaps by as much as ten-fold. The supply of gold and silver, which formed the basis of the monetary system, was unable to keep up with such rapid expansion. New sources of the precious metals were sought, and with Portuguese exploration, Africa soon became the major supplier of Europe's gold.

Slaves were also brought from Africa to fill the constant demand for labour, which had been in short supply since plagues had ravaged Europe. In preceding years, these plagues had reduced populations by as much as two-thirds. Indeed, by the end of the fifteenth century, slaves made up nearly ten percent of the population of Lisbon.

The insatiable demand for gold, silver, and slaves forced Europe to look beyond Africa, to Cathay. Spices such as pepper, cloves, nutmeg, cinnamon, and mace were required as well, not only to improve the flavour of meat but also to preserve it. Due to a lack of winter forage, farmers in Europe slaughtered most of their animals before the cold weather set in but, without spices, were unable to preserve meat throughout the long winter.

Pepper and cloves were in high demand, as they had become almost addictive, rather like coffee or tea today. These spices commanded high prices when they reached the open market in Europe, creating a potential for vast profits. Some idea of this potential can be gauged from records of sea voyages to the Spice Islands. In his circumnavigation of the globe at the end of the sixteenth century, Sir Francis Drake was away from England for three years. Yet despite this lengthy absence, as well as a shipwreck and the loss of half his cargo, he still made a profit on the voyage of 4,700 percent—due almost entirely to the sale of six tons of cloves at about five shillings a pound, between five and ten days' wages for a working man.

The high cost of spices in Europe was not related primarily to the dangers of trading. Many journeys had taken place across Asia since Marco Polo's return from Peking, and these had shown that the land routes were comparatively safe. Another cost factor was the complexity of transshipment. Caravans regularly made the trek but usually in short stages, in which goods were moved from one changeover to another by middlemen. Duties were charged at each stage, and as costs mounted, packages were shifted from camel trains to ponies to horse-drawn caravans and back to camels. Although middlemen were the cause of high prices, it was obviously impractical for Europeans to trade across land routes by themselves. The journey to Cathay and back was simply too long, and the European traveller had little control over his progress, being almost completely dependent on local inhabitants for guides and on animals for transport. Gradually it became clear that immense profits could be obtained by more direct trading, and the possibility of sea routes became more attractive.

Interest in this enterprise grew in the fifteenth century when the supply of spices and other goods reaching Europe from the East began to dry up. Gold sources became uncertain due to the vagaries of tribal wars. The Turks spread across Asia Minor and partially blocked the overland spice routes, and their war galleys also interrupted trade in the Mediterranean. Prices rose as supplies decreased. Merchants and princes alike were forced to look for alternative routes which would permit more direct contact with the East.

By the late fifteenth century Europe was in an ideal position to take part in ocean discovery. Ships had been developed which could sail a chosen line instead of wandering off course. They were tough enough to withstand the rigours of long sea voyages yet small enough to be financed privately rather than requiring the resources of large corporations or state funds. Perhaps just as importantly, the broadside cannon had been developed and was unsurpassed as a defence system. With this protection, Europeans had nothing to fear from ships of other nations, which were usually armed with only one gun in the prow and one in the stern.

Maps had also developed considerably from earlier days, and although mapmakers still worked on the basis of "where there be unknowns, place terrors," there were fewer terrors than before. The islands in the South Atlantic, the Azores, Madeira Islands and Canary Islands, had all been identified and were sufficiently well known to provide an embarkation point for longer voyages into the unknown. Psychologically, Europe had changed from the static society of the early Middle Ages to a bustling community with interchange of scholars, politicians and craftsmen. It was outward looking, individualistic, desperate for trade and had the added incentive of a militant religion intent on converting, or at least subjugating, the "heathen."

Exploration of Africa began in the early 1400s, when Prince Henry the Navigator established his observatory in southwest Portugal, and began to send out expeditions backed by the knowledge of his geographers, mathematicians and astronomers. Gradually the Portuguese spread down the west coast of Africa marking their progress with stone cairns. By 1473 they had crossed the equator, and by 1488 they had rounded the cape, originally called the Cape of Storms, but renamed Cape of Good Hope by John II. These expeditions prepared the way for Vasco da Gama's epic voyage, during which he rounded the Cape and pushed north to Mozambique before cutting across the Indian Ocean to Calicut on the Malabar coast of India.

Within a few years of Vasco da Gama's return to Lisbon in 1499, the Portuguese had established themselves as the dominant power in the Indian Ocean, partly due to the superiority of their naval gunnery and partly to their strength of purpose. Indeed, "strength" is perhaps too kind a word because they frequently forced the local inhabitants to trade with methods which would be abhorrent to modern sensibilities.

The ferocity of those early explorers is well illustrated by da Gama's treatment of a shipload of Moslem pilgrims who refused him a suitable tribute during his second voyage. He captured two large ships and twenty-two smaller vessels and, in the words of a Portuguese eye-witness, "cut off the hands and ears and noses of the crews and put all that into one of the smaller vessels.... He ordered their feet to be tied together as they had no hands with which to untie them; and in order that they should not untie them with their teeth, he ordered them [his crew] to strike upon their teeth with staves and they knocked them down their throats; and they were thus put on board, heaped upon the top of each other, mixed up with the blood which streamed from them; and he ordered mats and dried leaves to be spread over them, and the sails to be set for the shore, and the vessel set on fire; and there were more than 800 Moors, and the small vessel ... with all the hands and ears was also sent on shore under sail without being fired."[1]

There was obviously another side to the traditional picture of the brave Europeans sailing through uncharted waters for adventure and discovery!

The Portuguese were not the only ones interested in a sea route to Cathay, but their command of the western seas became so strong that in 1490, Ferdinand of Spain was persuaded to encourage Columbus to set forth across the Atlantic. Columbus had been thinking of the possibility of a western route to China as early as 1474 when he wrote to a Florentine scholar, Paolo Toscanelli. Toscanelli commented on Columbus's "magnificent and great desire to find a way to where the spices grow,"[2] and in reply to Columbus's letter he quoted an earlier

*Detail from the Catalan map of the world, drawn in 1375 for the King of France, showing a camel caravan taking the Polos on their Asian expeditions.* (Courtesy Bodleian Library, MS Bodley 264, f. 219)

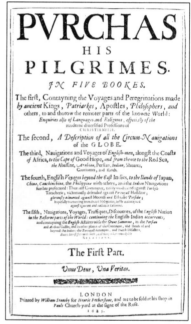

*The flyleaf of* Hakluytus Posthumus or Purchas His Pilgrimes *(London, 1625), assembled by English clergyman Samuel Purchas.*

A 1502 map of the world showing the territorial division set out by the 1494 treaty of Tordesillas between Spain and Portugal. Taken from a facsimile in "Sixteenth-Century Maps of Canada—A Checklist and Bibliography" (Ottawa, 1956). (Courtesy National Archives of Canada, NMC 17391)

til þe cum in to iiij. fadam deep and yf it be stremy
grounde it is betwene Hunsestant and calle in the entre
of the chanel of fflandres and soo goo youre cours
til ye have stvn fadam deep. than goo est northe est
a longe the see . + c̃.

*A painting of a late-fifteenth-century ship heaving the lead as it enters the English Channel.*
(Courtesy Pierpont Morgan Library, New York, M.775, f.138v)

*A symbolic engraving of the European explorer and his equipment: his ship, cannons, swivel guns, and navigational instruments.* (Courtesy National Maritime Museum, London)

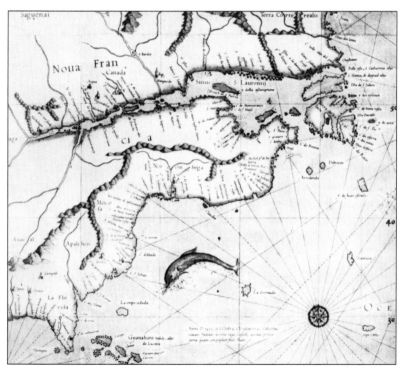

*Mercator's world map of 1569 showing part of the coastline of North America. This was the first projection in which a straight line drawn between two points gave the actual compass bearing.* (Courtesy Prins Hendrik Maritime Museum, Rotterdam)

authority, agreeing that the best route to Asia involved sailing west across the Atlantic. Toscanelli was mistaken in his estimation of the land mass of Asia,[3] and also the diameter of the earth. The result of these miscalculations led Columbus to believe that only 3,840 kilometres of ocean stretched between the Canary Islands and Japan, whereas the actual distance over land and water is almost 17,000 kilometres. Columbus also noted in his personal writings that he had visited Iceland in 1477, where he would almost certainly have learnt something of the North Atlantic and the lands to the west from the descendants of Viking settlers.

Columbus's plan for a voyage west was first presented to John II of Portugal, but was unsuccessful, probably because of Portugal's deep commitment to Africa and the East. After the Portuguese rounded the Cape of Good Hope in 1488, Columbus took his offer to King Ferdinand and Queen Isabella of Spain, while his younger brother, Bartholomew, was sent to England, and perhaps also to France. After long delays and initial refusals, Spain responded favourably but with little financial backing. The small port of Palos in Andalusia was instructed to build the caravalles *Niña* and *Pinta* at public expense, and Columbus himself chartered the *Santa Maria* from its owner, Juan de la Cosa.

Conditions on board the explorers' ships were primitive. The ships were small—the *Santa Maria*, of about 100 tons, carried 40 men, while the *Niña* and *Pinta*, each about 60 tons, carried only 25 each. These smaller caravelles were only about 21 metres long by 7 metres wide and were typical of most of the ships used on the longer expeditions. No sleeping accommodation was provided, except for the captain and master and possibly the officers. The men slept where they could, usually in the open. But the experience of the men varied enormously. Few were professional seamen, and sometimes nearly half the crew were boys. Indeed, on Columbus's fourth voyage, some members of his crew were only twelve and thirteen years old. Many countries impressed convicts who had been sentenced to death or banishment. These unfortunates were usually considered to be expendable. They would be used to test the intentions of hostile natives and were frequently cast ashore with some seeds and livestock in the rather vain hope that they might set up a watering station in case the ship ever returned.

Fleas, lice and rats were rife, and food was poor, although generally plentiful. Salted fish and meat did not keep well, and biscuits and grain quickly bred weevils. Worse still, the lack of fresh vegetables was responsible for outbreaks of scurvy. In the early 1600s, the English began to carry lime juice that provided the vitamin C required to prevent this fatal disease. Many died on longer voyages, and a death rate of one in five was not unusual on the long sea voyage to India. Surprisingly, there were few mutinies, and except for a few isolated instances, there were few captains who were unable to proceed as far as they wanted because of resistance from their crews.

Scurvy, the plague of the longer voyages, was a dreadful disease. According to one account, "it rotted all my gums which gave out a black and putrid blood. My knee joints were so swollen that I could not extend my muscles. My thighs and lower legs were black and gangrenous and I was forced to use my knife each day to cut into the flesh in order to release this black and foul blood. I also used my knife on my gums, which were livid and growing over my teeth. I went on deck each day ... holding a little mirror before me in my hand to see where it was necessary to cut. Then when I had cut away this dead flesh and caused much black blood to flow, I rinsed my mouth and teeth with my urine.... Many of our people died of it every day, and we saw bodies being thrown into the sea constantly, three or four at a time. For the most part they died with no aid given them, expiring behind some case or chest, their eyes and the soles of their feet gnawed away by the rats."[4]

It was in conditions like this that the great explorations took place, and it is hardly surprising that men became worried and uneasy when they had been out of sight of land for some time. Columbus took only thirty-three days to cross the Atlantic, but even then his sailors began complaining, and only his determination, combined with falsifications of the distance travelled each day (his faked figures were actually closer to the truth then those he calculated), persuaded them to continue. At last, on October 12, 1492, they sighted land in the Bahamas.

Spain moved quickly to exploit Columbus's discovery. A second voyage was approved without delay, almost as soon as he returned home. To forestall the interest of the Portuguese, negotiations were immediately begun with the Spanish Pope, Alexander VI, to ensure that the Spanish claim to the new lands would be valid throughout Christendom. Four Papal Bulls, highly favourable to Spain, were quickly issued from the Vatican. The first two granted all new lands discovered, or yet to be discovered by Columbus, to Spain. The third defined a Spanish sphere of influence, and set this to the west of a line drawn north to south through the Cape Verde Islands. The fourth Bull cancelled rights of discovery and occupation given to other nations in earlier Bulls. This was obviously of great concern to Portugal because it meant that Spain could claim rights in Asia if she reached Cathay travelling west before Portugal succeeded by the eastern route via Africa and the Indian Ocean. John II challenged the Pope's ruling, and following negotiation among the three parties, the issue was resolved in the Treaty of Tordesillas of 1494, which essentially divided the world between the two monarchies. In this treaty, the boundary was pushed west and a line was set "on the said ocean sea, from the Arctic to the Antarctic Pole. This boundary or line shall be drawn straight, as aforesaid, at a distance of three hundred and seventy leagues west of the Cape Verde Islands ... and all lands, both islands and mainlands, found and discovered already, or to be found and discovered hereafter, by the said King of Portugal ... towards the East ... shall belong to, and remain in the possession of, and pertain forever to, the said King of Portugal and his successors. And all other lands ... on the Western side of the same bound ... shall belong to, and remain in the possession of, and pertain forever to, the said King and Queen of Castille, Leon etc. and to their successors."[5] The treaty effectively set the dividing line at 46°37'W, thus giving the Americas to Spain but preserving Brazil for the Portuguese.

With the Spanish well in control in the New World and Portugal commanding the oceans around Africa and India, the sea routes to Cathay appeared closed to the other European nations. Henry VII of England had missed out on the opportunities of America when he turned down Columbus's offer in 1490, but only seven years later he commissioned a voyage by John Cabot, who also sailed west. Cabot sailed much farther north than Columbus and finished up on the east coast of Canada, but despite some further voyages, he found little of interest, except for the incredible fishing grounds on the Grand Banks of Newfoundland. These became the focus of an international fishery, but there were few other immediate developments, and it was not until the middle of the sixteenth century, in the Elizabethan Age, that the English began to exert themselves. Their impetus was partly envy of Spain and Portugal and partly greed, but there was a strong economic inspiration derived primarily from the failure of the English wool trade.

Wool was a mainstay of the English economy. In the time of Henry VIII, there were more sheep than people in the country. Sales ballooned and England became rich, but by 1550 new markets were being sought with the most potential being thought to lie in "the manifold islands of Japan and the northern part of China."[6]

With Spain and Portugal covering the southern routes, it was obvious that the English should look north, but whether east or west was not clear. Cabot had described the cold dark fogs of the western route, and so the first voyagers attempted to sail north and east around the European land mass. Most froze to death. Others became stuck in Russia, and it became clear that the route to Cathay must indeed be to the west. The search for this route by Englishmen such as Gilbert, Frobisher, Davis and Hudson gave England a major role in discovery in the North Atlantic. At the same time the French were also searching for a route to the East, primarily farther south, around the Gulf of St. Lawrence. Cartier's exploration of the St. Lawrence (1534-1541) opened up Canada to French settlement. Between 1499 and 1505, Portuguese from the Azores journeyed to Greenland and Labrador, while by 1540, Basque whalers had become well established in summer stations along the Strait of Belle Isle. But discovery in the North Atlantic had begun much, much earlier.

Before 1000 AD, Norse explorers, faced with mounting population pressures, had pushed west to Iceland and then on to Greenland. From there it was not far to Markland and Vinland, described in the

Norse sagas, both now well established in North America, although there is still some debate as to their exact location.

It is with these northerly voyages that this book is concerned. Not the voyages through warm seas to the sunbaked land of the South but, instead, the difficult and dangerous thrust through the cold waters of the North, between the icebergs and through the fogs. The voyages of the English, French, Basques and Portuguese are fairly well recorded. Details of Norse expeditions can be gleaned from the sagas and from recent archaeological work, and although written records are sparse, there can be no doubt that the Norse were in America well before the Spanish. But were they the first? Long before the Scandinavians, another small nation was sailing the northern seas along the western shores of the Atlantic. Irish monks of the sixth century travelled to and from Britain and had established communities in Iceland and perhaps farther north. There are hints in the Norse sagas that those monks reached Greenland, and there are intriguing possibilities that they journeyed west to the "Promised Land of the Saints." Whether they did, in fact, reach the shores of North America before Leif Eriksson can only be speculated upon, given the current state of knowledge. It is now quite clear, however, that there was no physical reason why they could not have made the voyage as early as the middle of the sixth century. In this matter, perhaps, readers can judge for themselves.

# CHAPTER ONE

# ST. BRENDAN
# AND THE IRISH

*T*hroughout the fifth and sixth centuries AD, Ireland was a country in transition. From a pagan, Celtic land, influenced by the Druids and their mystical rites, it was moving much more rapidly into the Christian era than Britain, its larger neighbour across the sea. Still a strongly Celtic culture, it received its first introduction to Christianity from St. Patrick. According to the traditional accounts, Patrick was captured at about the age of sixteen by Irish raiders during one of their many expeditions against the declining civilization of Roman Britain. Carried off to Ireland, he was enslaved for six years. He escaped, and following studies in Gaul and his consecration as Bishop, he returned to Ireland around 432 AD. He travelled widely, founding churches and ordaining bishops and priests until his death in 465. Historians query these dates, and suggest that his personal work was confined to a relatively small area. Nevertheless, there is little doubt that the church in Ireland grew considerably during his lifetime. Before he arrived, there were few Christians and only scattered churches. After his death the church was firmly established and organized, and paganism was well into its decline.

The country to which Patrick came was essentially pastoral and tribal in nature. Life centred on the family or small groups of families who came together under a clan system. Larger groups formed sub-kingdoms, and it was a natural progression for these eventually to come under the domination of a High King. By the fifth century, there were seven provincial kings under the nominal command of the High King at Tara, in County Meath.

Living conditions were extremely primitive, with humans and

animals sharing the same dwellings. Houses provided shelter from the rain and, to some degree, from the cold. Peat fires smouldered in a central hearth, and only some of the smoke percolated out through the open hole in the roof while the rest filled the room with its warm reek, keeping down the insects and covering the smell of refuse on the floor. Beds were almost non-existent, usually consisting of rush or heather piled on close-set flagstones laid on the bare earth at one side of the room—not very warm and not very comfortable.

Conditions among peasants were the most primitive, but the differences between theirs and those of their masters were more of degree than kind. The tribal society was highly structured, with at least three distinct classes. In addition to the peasantry at one end of the social scale and the land-owning warrior class at the other, there existed a middle class consisting of the educated and skilled. These were doctors and lawyers, as well as artists, poets, and musicians, who kept alive the traditional culture, as expressed in the folk tales and music, and, of considerable importance, the genealogy of their kings. Great respect was paid to these educated men, and despite the hard, short, and brutish life of the majority, there was a flowering of art and learning. Undoubtedly, this helped to preserve civilization in the British Isles throughout the Dark Ages, which descended after the Romans began to leave England in the early part of the fifth century.

The Celtic church was largely instrumental in keeping the flickering light of civilization alive in Ireland during these troubled times. Knowledge was passed from one priest to another. Manuscripts were written and illuminated, and historical records were kept. Patrick's conversions took place in the thirty or so years following his return to Ireland. By the time he died, he had founded the See of Armagh and had converted many of the petty chieftains and their subjects. Christianity became well established, and by the middle of the sixth century, Irish monks were leaving their country in ever-increasing numbers to spread the Gospel and to establish centres of Christianity in Britain and Europe.

In 563, one of the most famous of these missionaries, St. Columba, took his followers to the island of Iona, a small enclave on the west coast of Scotland. This became one of the primary centres of Christian civilization in northern Europe. From there he travelled north, quelling the Loch Ness monster on his way, to convert the northern Picts.

In later years the influence of his followers spread to the Orkney and Shetland islands, and possibly to the Faroe Islands and Iceland. Certainly, records show the Irish to have been in Iceland by 795.

Although he is the best known of these early missionaries, Columba was not alone in his travels. Columbanus set out for Gaul around 590, founding a number of monasteries between Luxeuil and Bobbio in Italy. His contemporaries ventured as far afield as Switzerland and Austria. St. Fiachra and St. Fursa were also in Gaul. St. Killan took the Word to Saxony, and St. Livinius was in the Netherlands. Wherever they went, they founded monasteries, and although most of the monastic traffic was between Ireland and England, a chain of monasteries eventually stretched from the British Isles right across Europe to Italy.

This was the heyday of Irish monasticism, and the era into which Brendan "the Navigator" was born, in or near Tralee, County Kerry, about 489 AD. His name is associated with monastic foundations in Clare, Galway and Kerry, but over time he became best known as the most adventurous voyager of all the Irish monks. Reports indicate that he sailed to Britain and Brittany in the south and to Iona, the Shetlands and the Orkneys in the north. But his most famous voyages, the ones which gave him the title the Navigator, are undoubtedly those described in the *Navigatio Sancti Brendani Abbatis*—the Voyage of St. Brendan—which tells marvellous tales of his voyages across the North Atlantic and describes his discovery of islands and continents to the west.[1]

The *Navigatio* was written in Latin, perhaps as early as 800, and is one of a whole series of similar writings referred to as the *Immrama*.[2] These invariably describe heroic voyages with a strong Christian element, and bear various similarities to one another. For many years there was argument and confusion over the validity of the *Navigatio*, the late date suggesting that it borrowed heavily from some of the other *Immrama*. There are now suggestions, however, that a primitive version of Brendan's voyage existed within a hundred years of his death. This version is thought to have influenced the *Voyage of Bran*,[3] written in the late sixth or early seventh century, which, in turn, is considered to have provided a foundation for the later *Voyage of Mael Duin*.[4]

Brendan's voyage is essentially a Christian allegory, but hidden among the miracles and the formalized writing are sound descriptions of the conditions which would be met by a small boat in the North Atlantic. Combined with details of the various landfalls which can be tentatively identified, these accounts have led many people to believe that Brendan actually reached the coast of North America. In medieval times, maps included "St. Brendan's Isle" far out in the Atlantic,[5] although usually to the south rather than to the north. As early as 1580, John Dee, astrologer, sorcerer, alchemist and mathematician, and Queen Elizabeth's geographer, used Brendan's Isle as a justification for England's claim to North America.

Certainly, although the journey would be arduous and hazardous in the extreme, it seems that there were no physical barriers to such a journey. It would, of course, have to have been done in easy stages with frequent landings to rest, make repairs and to replenish food and water supplies, but the boats used by the Irish monks were seaworthy and capable. They regularly travelled the stormy Irish Sea and were also capable of voyaging to the Shetland and Orkney islands.

The curragh, a small boat associated with Ireland, was in widespread use in Celtic areas of Britain, and indeed Caesar records it in use in the southwest of England. It was constructed with a wicker or wooden framework set between ribs which were covered in watertight animal hides stretched over the frame and sewn tightly together. The stern was drawn up more steeply than the bow, and although most curraghs were fairly small, larger ocean-going craft up to twelve metres long were used in later years for fairly regular sailings between Ireland, the Faroe Islands and Iceland. Capable of carrying a sail, these large craft bobbed along on top of the waves and thus were well suited to ocean travel. The larger curraghs died out in the eighth and ninth centuries, giving way to wooden construction in smaller versions. These were the coracles, useful for inshore and coastal work but able to carry only small quantities of goods, or one or two people, up and down the rivers and across estuaries.

In the *Navigatio*, Brendan is described as setting up his tent at the edge of the mountain "in a place called St. Brendan's seat, at a point where there was entry for only one boat." There, he and his followers set to work "and constructed a light boat ribbed with wood and with a wooden frame, as is usual in these parts. They covered it with ox-hides tanned with the bark of oak and smeared all the joints with the hides on the outside with fat. They carried into the boat hides for the makings of two other boats, supplies for forty days and other things needed for human life. They also placed a mast in the middle of the boat and a sail and the other requirements for steering a boat."

Setting out westwards at the time of the summer solstice, they spent the next seven years at sea roaming the Atlantic in search of the "Promised Land of the Saints." This land, an island, had been described to them by St. Barrind, who arrived one day at Brendan's monastery of Clonfert in East Galway. With tears in his eyes, he described this miraculous island to them, a land where no food or drink was necessary for subsistence, where there was never night and where there were "no plants which had not flowers nor trees which had not fruit."

During their voyages in search of God's island, Brendan's crew met with many monsters and miracles, and their tale is ritualized in the normal fashion of the *Immrama* and other early Christian allegories. The numbers three (for the Trinity) and twelve (for the Apostles) occur throughout. On many occasions Brendan sailed "for forty days," which really only means for a long time. There are cycles in the tale: fish are said to lie with their heads touching their tails in perfect circles; descriptions of the promised land at the beginning of the text are repeated at the end; Brendan and his followers return every year to the same spot for the celebration of Easter and Christmas. In all these respects, the narrative is stylized and ritualistic, yet behind the ritual, the monsters and the miracles, the reader forms the impression that the author is perfectly familiar with the North Atlantic. He understands the problems of sailing a small ship under Atlantic conditions, and perhaps most intriguing, he seems to be familiar with the lands and islands which might be encountered on a staged crossing.

After leaving Clonfert, Brendan, according to the *Navigatio*, drifted north for "forty days" until the wind dropped and he arrived at an island which bears a remarkable likeness to St. Kilda in the Western Hebrides. The island was "rocky and high," with "cliffs like a wall," and they spent three days circling the island before finally managing to land in a narrow vertical cut in the rock, the only suitable landing place. From there they sailed to the "Island of Sheep," where they arrived on the Thursday before Easter. This island was covered in white sheep "so numerous that the ground could not be seen." There they celebrated Good Friday and met a steward who supplied them with bread for the service and who was eventually to guide them to the promised land. Easter Saturday was spent on a nearby island— small and bare, there was no grass, only stones and some driftwood. While the brothers prayed, Brendan stayed in the boat, "for he knew what sort of Island it was." In the morning, after boiling their cauldron over an open fire, they were amazed to find the island beginning to move. Everyone would have been lost, but Brendan saved them and "threw each one of them into the boat by his hands." As they set sail, "the island" moved out to sea and their fire was still visible at a distance of two miles. Brendan then explained to his followers that the island was, of course, a whale, although he describes it as "a fish—the foremost of all that swims in the ocean," and goes on to explain jokingly that "he is always trying to bring his tail to meet his head but cannot because of his length. His name is Jasconius."

Their next port of call was on another nearby island, described as the "Paradise of Birds" and populated by white birds. One of them, being able to speak, reminded the brothers that they had now been one year away from home and prophesied that it would take them another six years before their search for the promised land was completed. The bird also told them that each year they would celebrate the Easter feasts on the Island of Sheep, the back of Jasconius, and the Paradise of Birds, and that they would soon find an island, the Community of

Saint Ailbe, on which they would pass each Christmas. Brendan then stayed on the Island of Birds until just after Pentecost—seven weeks after Easter.

It has been suggested that, at this point, Brendan was well north of Ireland, probably in the Faroe Islands, with their profusion of sheep, birds (white gulls and terns) and whales. Indeed, the word "Faroes" is based on a Danish word meaning "sheep," and in the early ninth century, an Irish writer, Dicuil, described the islands as swarming "with innumerable sheep and an amazing number of sea-fowl."[6] The sheep were said to have been brought to the islands by early Celtic colonists and to have proliferated there on "the small islands separated by narrow sounds on which for a hundred years dwelt hermits who came from our fatherland." The *Navigatio*'s description of the sheep, white birds, and islands not too far from one another is remarkably similar to Dicuil's description written several hundred years later.

When Brendan left the Island of Birds, his boat drifted south, and after only three months they reached the Community of Saint Ailbe. There they remained until after Christmas, spending their time with monks who had originally been led to the island by St. Ailbe. Three months—the duration of the voyage to Ailbe—is the longest time given for any single journey in the *Navigatio,* and it is perhaps significant that no mention is made of bad weather during this voyage. At that time of year, between June and December, good weather at sea over such a prolonged period would almost certainly preclude their movement in any direction other than south. This by itself is highly speculative. Other factors, however, also suggest southern waters. Not long after leaving Ailbe, Brendan drifted to an island having bad water which "lies heavily upon your bodies." Close by, about three days' sail away, he came to a part of the sea which was coagulated "like a thick curdled mass." Taken together, these suggest he had sailed down to the Azores, where he landed first at Madeira before drifting with the prevailing winds to St. Michaels, with its many sulphurous springs and "bad" water, and then on to the Sargasso Sea. From there they followed "a wind favourable to them from west to east" (perhaps in the Gulf Stream) before arriving back at the Island of Sheep in time for

Easter. All of this may seem quite vague, but current and wind directions, together with the description of the island with bad water (there are relatively few in the Atlantic) and the "curdled" sea, tend to fit the locations suggested. There is also evidence to suggest that from a very early age, the Irish were familiar with the Gulf Stream, drifting in from the west. Certainly, this current, and its offerings of exotic driftwood and other things (including the occasional non-European corpse!), was sufficiently familiar to the Irish for Columbus to have referenced St. Brendan's notebooks, even though no published account of this current existed. But there are also tentative suggestions in the tenth-century *Immrama*, known as *Snedgus*, of a warm current to the northwest of Britain, and it is not at all unreasonable to suggest that the Irish travellers of Brendan's time were familiar with this current.

Once again, Brendan and his followers celebrated Easter, and once more they were reminded that they must travel between the islands of Sheep and Birds at Easter and to the Community of Saint Ailbe for Christmas, until their "seven years and great and varied trials" came to fruition by finding the "Promised Land of the Saints." It is from that point that the *Navigatio* begins to document some of the trials and peculiarities of the voyage and ceases to provide detailed annual descriptions as the monks voyage north and south between their two primary anchor points.

Soon after leaving the Island of Birds, they fell in with a sea monster. Here it should be emphasized that Brendan's ox-hide boat was only a few metres long, so a "sea monster" would not need to be very large to be quite terrifying. The *Navigatio* describes it as being of tremendous size and records it snorting foam from its nostrils, while ploughing through the waves at great speed. The incident is also recorded in the *Life of St. Brendan*, possibly completed in the twelfth century.[7] Here the monster is described as a "sea cat," and is obviously a walrus with its "hugh eyes, bristles and tusks like a boar." This account also describes two black fiends who have been tentatively associated with the "Skraelings" of the Norse sagas, and the inference is that Brendan is again in the high latitudes.

The boat is saved from the sea cat by another monster, which speeds in from the west and kills it. After finding part of the carcass washed ashore on a tree-covered island, they gathered the meat because Brendan had predicted they would remain on the island for a long time. Sure enough, bad weather held them there for three months before they set off again.

Before again spending Christmas on the Community of Saint Ailbe, Brendan visited an area which might well describe parts of the West Indies. The island they landed on "was extremely flat, so much so that it seemed to them to be level with the sea. It had no trees or anything that would move in the wind," but "was covered with white and purple fruit." On another island they found fruit "all of equal size and like a large ball," each one giving a pound of juice. On yet another island the air had a "perfume like that of a house filled with pomegranates," and the land was so fertile "that all the trees were bent down to the ground" under the weight of fruit. In the same area, in the following year, they passed through a sea so clear that they could see "different types of fish lying on the sand below. It even seemed that they could touch them with their hands so clear was the sea." The flat (coral?) island, profusion of growth, perfumed air, and clear sea all suggest tropical waters, quite different from descriptions of the northern seas which follow after they again sailed north.

"One day when they had finished their Masses, a pillar in the sea appeared to them." It took three days to sail up to the pillar, which was enormously tall and made of "bright crystal, harder than marble." This, presumably, was an iceberg. As they tried to get close, they found it was surrounded by a "mesh" which may have been loose pack-ice. Manoeuvring their boat through this "net" to examine the pillar at close range, they spent the next four days taking measurements around its perimeter. After that they began to row north and, once past the "net," hoisted the sail and travelled north for the next eight days. At that time they found a rocky island "full of slag and without trees or grass, full of smiths' forges." Brendan was "troubled about this island" and decided not to go ashore. However, there were onshore winds blowing, and as they attempted to sail past the island, they were

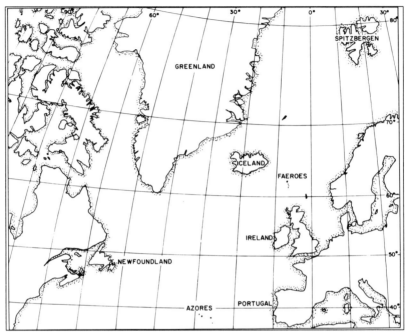

*General outline of the North Atlantic.* (Drawing by Terry Dyer)

*An early woodcut of St. Brendan and his monks on their way to the earthly paradise. Their boat is surrounded by Jasconius, the whale which is always trying to catch its tail.* (Courtesy Universitats-bibliothek Heidelberg, Cod. Pal. Germ. 60, f.1, 179v)

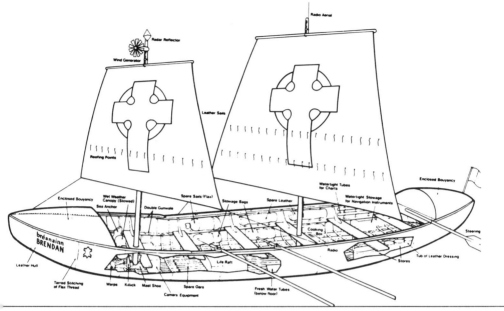

*Sketch of the modern* Brendan, *based on the sixth-century style and used by Timothy Severin for his voyage retracing the possible route of St. Brendan.*
(Courtesy *Canadian Geographic*)

Left: *An early ogham stone in County Kerry, Ireland. The slanting lines carved across the sharp vertical edges of the stone give the genealogy and name of a local hero.* (Courtesy *Canadian Geographic*)

Right: *The basis of the ogham (early Irish) script. It consists of differing numbers of slanting or horizontal lines drawn across a vertical, often the edge of a standing stone.* (Courtesy *Canadian Geographic*)

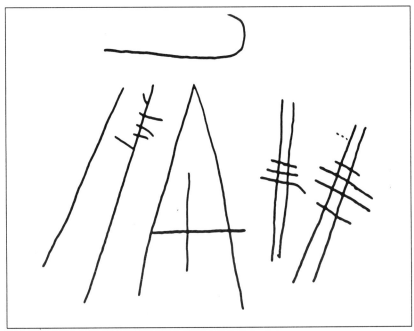

*Typical inscriptions on the ogham stone found at St. Lunaire. When lichen was removed, the sharpness of the lines indicated that they had been cut with iron or steel rather than with flint knives, used by early Indians. (Courtesy* Canadian Geographic*)*

Bottom (facing page), above: *Woodcut illustrations of St. Brendan's voyage, from a German translation of the* Navigatio *(Ulm, 1499). The scenes show the monks' encounter with a siren, a holy man floating on the sea, and a sea monster.*
(Courtesy Trustees of the British Museum)

blown close inshore, where they could hear the smiths hard at work with "the bellows blowing, as if it were thunder, and the blows of hammers on iron and anvils." Brendan prayed for deliverance, but he had hardly finished his prayer when one of the inhabitants—"very shaggy and full at once of fire and darkness"—appeared from the forge. Seeing the boat, he ran back and reappeared "carrying tongs in his hands that held a lump of burning slag of immense size and heat. He immediately threw the lump on top of the servants of Christ but it did no hurt to them. It passed more than 200 yards above them. Then the sea where it fell, began to boil.... The smoke rose from the sea as from a fiery furnace." Fortunately the brothers were able to row clear and, after they were about a mile away and out of danger, they looked back to see "the whole island ablaze, like one big furnace, and the sea boiled just as a pot full of meat boils when it is well plied with fire. All day long they could hear a great howling from the island ... and the stench of fire assailed their nostrils."

On "another day" they came yet again to a high mountain, this one being "very smoky on top." One of the brothers was snatched away from the group by "a multitude of demons" and could not rejoin them, as the wind changed to carry the boat to the south. "When they looked back from a distance at the island, they saw that the mountain was no longer covered with smoke, but was spouting flames from itself up to the ether and then breathing back, as it were, the same flames again upon itself. The whole mountain from the summit right down to the sea looked like one big pyre."

These descriptions of islands in flame and flying lumps of slag are evocative of volcanic eruptions which, the *Navigatio* relates, were to the north of "the pillar of crystal," and were therefore probably in the subarctic regions. Iceland, or perhaps even Jan Mayen Island to the north, would seem to fit these descriptions quite well, being highly volcanic and also in northern latitudes.

After sailing to the south, they came upon the Island of Paul the Hermit, where "they could not find a landing place because of the height of the cliff. The island was small and circular, about two hundred yards in circumference. There was no earth on it, but it looked like a naked rock like flint." The island of Rockall lies at about the same latitude as St. Kilda, approximately two hundred miles west of it, and might well fit this description. Rockall is very small, being no more than one hundred feet or so wide at its widest point, the cliffs rising almost vertically from the sea, with no suitable landing spot. Indeed, it is impossible to land at all, except in the calmest possible sea, and Brendan's crew managed to get ashore only by finding a gap in the rock which was so small that "it could scarcely take the prow of the boat." Brendan and his men were now near the end of their seven-year adventure. As foretold, they arrived back at the Island of Sheep on Easter Saturday, to be met by the steward, who joined them when they left in the evening. Jasconius, the whale, was found in his usual place, and as usual, they moved on to the Island of Birds, where they remained until the eighth day of Pentecost. Then, with the bird's blessing and the steward's guidance, they set off for the promised land.

This time, according to the *Navigatio*, "their voyage was for forty days towards the east," at which point a "great fog enveloped them, so that one of them could hardly see the other." They were told that the fog encircled the island they were looking for, and after sailing through the mist for an hour, "a mighty light shone all around them again and the boat rested on the shore."

This is one of the most intriguing parts of the *Navigatio* because, apart from the direction given, east rather than west, the description suits the island of Newfoundland perfectly. Located just north of the mouth of the St. Lawrence River, Newfoundland sits at the junction of the warm Gulf Stream and the cold Labrador Current. As these two ocean currents mix together on the Grand Banks, off Newfoundland's rocky coastline, fogs develop and spread widely. The fog, however, is a typical sea fog sitting on the surface of the water and only a few hundred feet thick. It penetrates the bays and estuaries of the island, but in the summer and fall, the sun will be shining strong and bright as soon as a boat reaches the land and moves out of the mist. Nevertheless, the *Navigatio* says clearly that Brendan sailed east rather than west, and this is a stumbling block. There may well have been an error in transcription at some time, in which case there would be little problem in identifying Newfoundland as the Promised Land of the Saints; on the other hand, the fog described may have been only a mystical, magical fog hiding the island from unbelievers. The *Navigatio* indicates that the island is well to the west of Ireland, but there is little indication of how far. At the very beginning of the story, St. Barrind first describes the island to Brendan, telling him of the "delightful Island" three days' sail from Ireland and how, from there, he had journeyed west where he found the same fog that had enveloped Brendan's boat. No mention, however, is made of distances or time, for the journey and most other parts of the story tie in with the idea that the promised land is far to the west of Ireland.

The exact location probably does not matter too much. Transcriptional errors are not unknown, and there is every possibility that the original text said "west" rather than "east." This would be in keeping with the overall thrust of the *Navigatio*, which is generally descriptive of events and places to the west of Ireland, most of them a long way (forty days' journey). However, the overall impact of the story of Brendan's voyage is just as important as the details, and certainly more important than pinpointing exact locations. What comes across clearly is the author's familiarity, however obtained, with the types of landfalls which might be made in the Northwest Atlantic, together with some knowledge which is highly reminiscent of the South. He knows about the steep cliffs and the small rocky inlets. He is aware of the profusion of sheep and sea birds. Fog, perhaps off the coast of Newfoundland, icebergs and pack-ice drifting down from Greenland, volcanoes in Iceland, and the arctic monsters of the North all feature in the story.

If this were all, it would not be too convincing. However, there is significant evidence from other sources to suggest that the Irish moved north and west to colonize the North Atlantic, and there are hints that they might have moved as far west as America.

The written evidence comes from two sources. In 825, Dicuil, an Irish monk, wrote the *Liber de Mensura Orbis Terrae*, in which he describes the seas around Ireland, together with numerous islands.[8] Although he says that some of these are to the south of Britain and others to the west, they are "most numerous in the north-western sphere and to the north." Dicuil relied on only hearsay of some of these islands, but states that he had visited a number of them and had actually spent some time living on others. One of the islands he describes is clearly in the high latitudes because he notes that in the height of the summer the sun remained in the sky throughout almost the entire night, and it stayed bright enough at midnight "to clean oneself of lice!" Only one day's sail north of this island the sea was frozen. Dicuil claims that Irish monks had lived on the island for thirty years, and certainly this was far in advance of any Norse settlement in the area. It seems probable that he was referring, once again, to Iceland, and the Norse sagas, discussed in the next chapter, do indeed confirm the presence of the Irish in Iceland before it was settled by the Norse adventurers. Brendan's *Navigatio* suggests, and this is also confirmed by Norse writings, that the monks may have voyaged much farther. Whether they did or not, there is now no doubt that such journeys were possible for a group of sixth-century monks sailing in curraghs made of animal skins.

For many years, one of the main criticisms of the *Navigatio* was that the voyages described would have been quite impossible under the circumstances which existed in the fifth and sixth centuries. No one believed that a transatlantic journey could be made in a boat covered in animal skins even if the journey was taken in easy stages round the land masses of the North.

This supposition was shattered in 1976 when five men led by Tim Severin sailed a thirty-six-foot open, leather-skinned curragh from the British Isles to the coast of North America. Leaving Ireland in May, they took sixty days to reach Iceland, where they stopped for the winter before setting off once again in May 1977, to arrive off the coast of Newfoundland on June 26. Severin and his crew followed the pattern of the *Navigatio*, north to the Faroe Islands and Ireland, and then west past the southern tip of Greenland, and down to Newfoundland. Not only did their voyage prove the possibilities of a similar voyage 1,400 years ago, it also provided convincing confirmation that the author, or authors, of the *Navigatio* was fully conversant with the problems and difficulties of sailing curraghs in the North Atlantic. He knew, for example, as Severin says, "that it is impossible to row up-wind in a boat which sits so high in the water that a foul wind blows you down on a hostile shore however much you want to get clear."[9] The description of how Brendan's large curragh beached and how the monks dragged it out of the surf and up shallow streams with tow ropes seemed "wholly authentic." When they came close to Newfoundland, the modern *Brendan* ran into pack ice and the crew manhandled their craft past the large floes and the small "bergy bits" in much the same way that the original *Brendan* was manoeuvred through the mantle net surrounding the pillar of crystal. Even the *Navigatio's* brief comments on crew and boat construction took on a new significance after Severin's voyage. *Brendan's* crew numbered fourteen, which, according to Severin, was a sensible number. He found his own crew of only four or five to be far too few to cope safely with the problems they encountered.

Initially there was considerable skepticism about the ability of a skin boat to withstand the rigours of the North Atlantic. However, Severin built his craft using only traditional materials and techniques and found it ideally suited to the journey. The ribs of the *Brendan*, made of ash from County Longford, were covered with forty-nine ox-hides tanned in a solution of oak bark at a traditional tannery in Cornwall— one of the few places still capable of doing this work. The hides were sewn with over 20,000 stitches of hand-rolled flax thread, and the whole was well smeared with wool grease, which "gave off a stench no human body could equal" but which interestingly "acted as a magnet for the whales ... [which] ... would surface beside us, circle us, or even lie gently beneath our hull."[10]

From the moment of launching, the medieval design showed its capability of dealing with the conditions of the voyage. The hull "flexed to the waves" and was "tuned to the motion of the sea." As the voyage progressed, the condition of the hull, far from weakening, actually improved. "Daily inspection revealed that although the leather had become saturated with seawater, weeping a fine continual dew on its inner surface, the increasing cold made the oxhide stiffer and stronger."[11] Like St. Brendan, Tim Severin took spare oxhides with him and found them essential to his crossing. Off the coast of eastern Greenland they ran into a storm and would most probably have foundered without the spare hides to act as a wave deflector. Leather patches were also necessary when the *Brendan* was holed by ice. Heavy pack-ice caused relatively little damage and resulted in only one 10-centimetre tear, despite the ice being so thick that the Canadian Coast Guard later admitted that they had little expectation of the boat getting through safely.

Severin's voyage does not prove that St. Brendan journeyed the whole way across the North Atlantic, but he has proved that it was possible. Indeed, not only did he show the possibility of the voyage, he also showed that it would have taken place very much as it is described in the *Navigatio*. The northerly route has stopping places at distances well within the capabilities of a large curragh, and the handling of Severin's curragh bears remarkable resemblance to descriptions in the *Navigatio*.

There is yet one more piece of evidence which must be considered. In November 1974, while Severin was preparing for his voyage, two Canadian archaeologists discovered what has become known as the ogham stone.[12] Robert McGhee and James Tuck were on the Great Northern Peninsula, in the northwest of Newfoundland, doing some field work near the Norse settlement at L'Anse aux Meadows when their guide asked them if they wanted to see "the stone with writing on it." This was well known to the villagers of St. Lunaire, nearby, and proved to be a large boulder about the size of a small car, with a patch of lichen on one end beneath which were "shallow lines which someone had long ago cut with a sharp tool." The lichen covering the inscription provided good evidence of its age. At some time in the past, a small oval-shaped area of the main inscription—there were three in all—had been scraped clear and lichens had regrown. Fortunately, the lichen which had colonized this area grows from a central point and spreads in a circular pattern. It was, therefore, possible to estimate the age of the lichen colony at at least 150 to 200 years, giving an indication of a minimum age of the carving. However, two more inscriptions were found on the same boulder, both of which were more heavily encrusted with lichens than was the main inscription.

19

The inference, assuming they were all done at the same time, is that the main inscription was cleared at some time long after the carvings were cut, but at least 150 to 200 years ago. From the shape and style of the markings, McGhee and Tuck concluded that they had all been made by the same hand, probably at the same time. Furthermore, the clarity and fineness of the lines indicated the use of a steel tool, and the heavy lichen growths on the secondary inscriptions led them to believe that they were very old, certainly predating the Basques or French landings in the sixteenth and eighteenth centuries.

What was particularly surprising, however, was the nature of the inscriptions. The carvings appeared to be some form of writing but were obviously not based on the Roman or Runic alphabets, which have been used in western countries and Scandinavia for 2,000 years. Instead, the St. Lunaire inscriptions consisted of a series of small incised straight lines running across a number of central vertical lines. These marks are strongly reminiscent of an alphabet called "ogham" which was used by the Druid and early Christian inhabitants of Ireland but about which very little is known. The few surviving examples of the script tend to be on ancient memorial stones where one corner serves as the central line. It is not known whether the script developed in Ireland or whether it was developed elsewhere in pre-Roman Celtic areas of Europe.

McGhee and Tuck sent photographs of the inscriptions to epigraphers with an interest in deciphering ancient inscriptions on rocks, burial stones and coins. The reactions were varied and somewhat inconclusive. Some amateur epigraphers had no difficulty in identifying the carvings as ogham and even managed to translate the clearest inscriptions as "Mag," meaning "land" or "plain," or "Maq," meaning "son of." Others, among them experts on ancient Irish writings, were less confident and found the inscriptions to be unintelligible, bearing only "an interesting, but distant, resemblance to ogham inscriptions from the old world." One enthusiast immediately recognized the St. Lunaire writing as ogham script but stated that it was not Irish in origin, belonging rather to the Celtic inhabitants of the Iberian Peninsula during the first millennium BC!

Despite these differences, there seems little doubt that the inscriptions are very old. Forgeries of rock carvings are not uncommon, but the lichen growth would indicate that if it were a forgery, it was done more than two hundred years ago by someone who had at least a passing acquaintance with a script which died out in the fifth century and was not rediscovered until the twentieth! This seems unlikely. However, the heavy lichen growth on the other inscription suggests a much older age, prior to the Basque visits, and the shape and detail of the carvings indicate the use of steel tools which would imply a European, rather than a native North American, origin. The evidence suggests the creator could be a man of education and Irish background, but whether he was an Irish monk on a voyage like Brendan's, or one of the "Papar" who disappeared from Iceland, or perhaps a slave taken by the early Norse settlers on their journey to Markland and Vinland, can never be ascertained. Even these explanations may be stretching credulity, and it is possible, although it seems unlikely, that the inscriptions are no more than mindless carvings which just happen to bear a resemblance to ancient Irish writing.

Individually these accounts could be, and indeed have been, treated with considerable skepticism. However, when they are taken together, the strength and credibility of the whole is, as usual, much greater than that of the individual parts. The *Navigatio*'s descriptions of what are possibly Iceland, the Faroe Islands, Newfoundland and other islands in the Atlantic, together with its accounts of cruising whales, fierce walruses, ice pillars, pack ice and coastal fogs off the shores of North America, are less coincidental and more acceptable.

Tim Severin's journey across the northern part of the Atlantic in a curragh, designed and built to the standards of the Dark Ages, totally countered suggestions that St. Brendan's voyage was impossible. By itself, this would have been a big step forward, but Severin's expedition achieved much more because it also showed that the descriptions in the *Navigatio* were eminently reasonable. The traditional and natural materials used to build his boat stood up to the rigours of the voyage far better than modern materials. Descriptions of the seagoing qualities of a large curragh proved to be accurate, and the route across the

North, with its several landfalls, was certainly the only one possible for such a craft. Having made the journey himself, Tim Severin has written of his personal conviction that the author of the *Navigatio* had first-hand experience of the conditions and the places he was describing. Finally, there is the coincidence of the discovery of rock inscriptions in Newfoundland, the island where St. Brendan may have landed and where the Norse almost certainly did land.

None of this proves that any Irish monks, or even St. Brendan in particular, did discover or make a landfall in North America, but it at least proves that it was possible for them to have done so. If the magical and ritualized parts of the *Navigatio* are discounted, what remains is, in essence, a story of exploration and adventure. None of the places visited is clearly located, but the descriptions are such that many can be tentatively identified. If, on the basis of the other evidence, these hints are taken at their face value, it is possible to make a very good case that the Irish were the first Europeans to visit the New World. At least, the possibility seems, like the *Navigatio*, to be eminently reasonable.

CHAPTER TWO

# *THE VIKING EXPLOSION*

While there may be considerable doubt regarding the achievements of the early Irish monks, there can be little doubt about the exploits of the Vikings, although the written evidence is hardly more reliable. The Norse sagas are not dissimilar to the Irish *Immrama*, are certainly more founded in fact, and are more related to actual historical figures, while nevertheless including much that is fanciful and imaginary. The difference between the two is that the stories described in the sagas are borne out by evidence in the stones. Archaeological excavations in Iceland, Greenland and in North America have found beyond doubt that there was a Viking presence in each of these areas. People lived, built houses and farms, and died, and as they did so, the record of their lives was clearly written in the remains of their dwellings and in the things they left behind.

The Viking Age covers approximately 325 years, between about 760 AD and 1080 AD. The explosion of the Vikings from Denmark, Sweden and Norway into an unsuspecting Europe began essentially with a surprise attack at Lindisfarne in 787. The monastery at Jarrow, on the same coast, was raided in 794, and the one at Iona, on the west coast of Scotland, in 795. "The ravaging of heathen men destroyed God's church at Lindisfarne through brutal robbery and slaughter," wrote one of the monks.[1] For a generation, the Vikings turned their attention to Irish and Continental coasts, returning again in 835. Usually their raids were quick strikes. They landed suddenly at a coastal site, plundered the nearby village or monastery and left again quickly, seldom penetrating more than eighteen kilometres inland. By the middle of the ninth century, however, the pattern had changed,

23

and more organized raids took place with the intention of conquering the people and forming settlements. Eventually the Vikings became well established on both sides of the English Channel, in Normandy under Rolo, and in England under King Cnut (Canute), the first Danish king over the whole of England.

Although the British Isles suffered severely because of their proximity to the Norse countries, the raids were only one aspect of the Viking explosion. Navigating south to continental Europe, they ravaged the shores of Normandy and Holland, but also sailed up the Seine to attack Paris, and south to fight in Spain. Most of the voyages to Britain and southern Europe were designed as raiding voyages, to plunder or to obtain land for settlement. The Vikings were also great traders and journeyed east, marching across Russia and sailing downriver to Byzantium. They also moved west, setting up colonies in Iceland and Greenland, and then travelling to the shores of North America.

By and large, it was the Danes who moved south to attack and then conquer parts of Britain and continental Europe. Swedes marched east, trading and raiding as they went, but motivated primarily by trade. Men from Norway also sailed south, like the Danes, attacking Scotland and founding independent kingdoms in the Western Isles. On the way, they put down settlements in the Shetland, Orkney and Faroe islands. As their horizons expanded, they spread west in epic voyages to Iceland, Greenland and beyond.

No independent Viking nation existed. Instead, there were various tribal groups bound together by a common language and common beliefs. The Vikings were pagans in a Christian world, united by their worship of gods such as Odin and Thor. Society was organized around districts, each with its own assembly of free landowners called the "thing." There were noblemen, and kings might be set up over a number of provinces. These ruled by hereditary right, but were also subject to elections to determine if they were worthy to rule.

While it is usually reckoned that conversion to Christianity brought an end to the Viking Age, the reasons for its beginnings are not so clear. A large part of the cause of this outpouring of men and ships was related to a burgeoning population and a severe hunger for land. The

Vikings were primarily farmers, and it would be wrong to think of them only as ferocious fighters. Most took no part in the savage raids on the monasteries around the coast of Britain; those who did spent only a small part of their life doing so. By and large, the Vikings were a pastoral people who needed land for their cattle and other livestock. When land was not available, an alternative was required, particularly for the hot-headed and high-spirited landless youths who needed to find some way of making their fortunes.

This need for space occurred among a people who were, above all else, consummate sailors. The coastline of Norway alone, not counting the bays and fjords, is more than 2,500 kilometres long. There are some 16,000 islands, and the land is penetrated by deep and winding fjords. Although most of the country is above the Arctic Circle, the waters are warmed by the Gulf Stream, and travel by water is generally easier than over land. This had been true since as far back as the Bronze Age, and since then, Viking shipwrights had raised the art of ship-building to a high level. They had learned how to use sails, and their ships were light open vessels capable of speeds up to twenty knots. For their time, they were the best ships in Europe. With these ships, the Vikings obtained a control of the seas unparalleled until the European nations began to expand across the globe, nearly four hundred years later, having similarly developed ships (and armaments) to the stage where long ocean voyages became possible.

One of the best, and best-known, examples of the Viking longship was excavated from a burial mount at Gokstad in Norway. Constructed entirely of oak and measuring about twenty-three metres long by about five metres wide, it is relatively narrow and highly manoeuvrable. The shallow draft, typical of Viking raiding vessels, was designed to give them easy access to land. The ship was very flexible and this, perhaps like Brendan's curragh, made it particularly suited to the rigours of the North Atlantic. In 1893, a replica was sailed from Bergen to Newfoundland in twenty-eight days. The gunwale flexed and twisted, but the boat remained watertight.

Power was provided primarily by a woolen sail hoisted on ropes and fixed to a central mast, which may have been about eleven metres long. A rudder fixed to the side of the ship gave directional stability, and oars were provided for manoeuvring and emergency or when the ship was becalmed. The origin of the name of the men themselves, the Vikings, is not clearly understood but is thought to relate to "taking turns at rowing."

Other ships which were wider and deeper have also been excavated. These, the *hafskip* or *knorr*, were ocean-going cargo ships. Their speeds were much slower, perhaps only five to six knots, but they were better suited to open-ocean voyages. With central holds capable of carrying perhaps 15 to 20 tons of goods in a space of about 35 cubic metres, these ships, it is thought, sustained the Viking colonies in Iceland and Greenland. None of them, however, were particularly comfortable. There was no dry closed-in accommodation, and a long sea voyage, whether with colonists or on a raiding expedition, must have involved considerable hardship and discomfort.

The Vikings had no understanding of longitude, but, like the early European sailors who came after them, they could hold a course on a fixed latitude. As well, they had an enormous stock of information regarding currents, fish, birds, sea mammals, driftwood and seaweed. The Vikings also understood the art of dead reckoning and had a good knowledge of the stars. With Norway's long coastline and its innumerable islands and inlets, they were used to coastal sailing and the necessity of identifying and remembering landmarks. Once Iceland and Greenland had been discovered, it was not too difficult to follow landmarks up the coast of Norway to the correct latitude (north of the Faroe Islands and just south of the Arctic Circle) and then to sail west on that latitude until Iceland came into view. Greenland could be reached in the same way, by starting off farther to the south, just north of Bergen. This would take the ship past the south of Iceland and bring Greenland into sight in about fourteen days. Throughout the voyage the Captain would have a rough idea of his location, based not on a measure of the distance travelled, but on the state of the currents, the colours of the waters and the types of sea birds and mammals he saw as each day passed.

To help them on their longer voyages, when they were well out to sea, the Norse developed an ingenious method of determining the location of the nearest land. The extra visibility gained by climbing to the top of the mast was limited, so they used birds which were free to fly far above the ship. For a variety of reasons they chose to use ravens. These birds are strong fliers and, being large and black, are easily visible against a light sky or white clouds. When the captain wanted to calculate the distance to the nearest land, he would release a raven from its cage, and closely watch its progress. If it returned to the ship, no land was in sight; if it flew back towards their last landfall, he could conclude that they were still closest to it. If, however, the shortest distance to land was ahead of them, the raven would fly towards it, indicating the direction the ship should take, and that a few more days' sail would bring it into sight.

The Vikings probably learned of the existence of Iceland and the Faroe Islands during their savage attacks on the coast of Ireland, but perhaps naturally, no mention is made of this in the *Islendingabok*— "the Book of the Icelanders"—or the *Landnamabok*—"the book of the settlements"—the two main sources on the early settlement of Iceland. Both do, however, admit that "there were Christian men here then whom the Norsemen called 'papar.'" Details are given in the *Landnamabok* of Ari Marsson. Written about 1130 and describing events of the late tenth century, Marsson's *Landnamabok* clearly indicates: "... before Iceland was settled from Norway there were men there whom the Norse style 'papar.' These were Christians, and people considered that they must have come from the British Isles, because there were found left behind them Irish books, bells and croziers and other things besides, from which it might be deduced that they were Irishmen. It is recorded in English books at that time that there was trafficking to and fro between these countries." What happened to the "papar" is not clear because they disappeared from Iceland and are not mentioned again, except where the *Islendingabok* notes that "they went away because they were not prepared to live in heathen company." Where they went is a mystery. They may simply have retreated into the interior to live apart from "the heathens," or they may have returned to Ireland, but it is possible that they fled westwards in front of the Vikings to finish up in Greenland or farther west. In describing Ari Marsson's voyages in the late tenth century, the *Landnamabok* tells how he "was driven across the sea by heavy gales to Hvitramannaland, also called 'Great Ireland.' It lies westward in the sea near Vinland the Good. It is said that one can sail there from Ireland in six days. Ari could not escape thence and was baptized there. This was first told by Hrafni Hlymreksfari who had been long himself in Limerick in Ireland." The Viking adventurers of the eleventh century were well aware of Hvitramannaland, locating it close to Markland, now identified with the coast of Labrador. In later writings, there are hints that Irish monks were here before the Vikings, but the comments are few and indirect.

The "papar" left soon after the Vikings arrived in Iceland, around 860 AD. People settled quickly, and although the influx was stimulated largely by intense land hunger in the mother country, Norway, many left because of the apparent tyranny of King Harald Fairhair. Harald had imposed peace and order on a united Norway. Oaths of allegiance were required, internal feuding was put down, and taxes and tithes were to be paid. Many who saw this as a restraint on their freedoms left, and while Harald is viewed as wise and good by Norwegian history, he was quite the opposite to the early settlers of Iceland.

This state of affairs occurred in Norway just as the Vikings in Europe suffered a number of significant military reverses. At the end of the ninth century, Viking armies were thrown back by King Alfred and his sons in England, by the Irish kings who recaptured Dublin in 902, and by Britons and others in continental Europe. Retreating north, they found Harald's peaceful, ordered Norway of little interest and moved west.

Settlement of Iceland was fairly rapid, and by 930 AD, all of the habitable land, about one-sixth of the total, had been taken. By then there were between 40,000 and 50,000 inhabitants. According to tradition, the first "thing" was set up just to the north of the location of modern Reykjavik. Similar assemblies followed in different parts of the island, but they did not provide the system that was required. Soon it became clear that there was a need for a central government, and a single parliament, the "Althing," was inaugurated between 927 and 930 AD. This met for a two-week period in the summer on a grassy plain about forty-five kilometres north of Reykjavik. There the law would be debated and the people would gather to hear and to discuss the decisions. This was very important because the Viking idea of law was strongly related to the idea of open judgement by freely elected peers. Despite this democratic system, however, power remained very much in the hands of a few leading families whose will was accepted by virtue of their position and lineage. Still this fledgling republic, converted to Christianity around the year 1000 AD, survived for over three hundred years, until it disintegrated and was taken over by Norway between 1262 and 1264. Long before this, however, another emigration, this time from Iceland to Greenland, took place. It started with about 400 colonists, grew to around 5,000 and lasted for nearly five hundred years.

The move from a settled Iceland to Greenland and on to the shores of North America appears quite reasonable when looking at a map. The distances are no longer than the distance from Norway to Iceland, the latitudes are no higher, and the seas no worse. But the weather was not always good, and the sagas relate how Greenland was discovered accidentally by a sailor, Gunnbjorn Ulf-Krakuson, who was blown off course and "storm-driven west across the ocean." His discovery was not followed up for fifty years until Eirikr Thorvaldsson, nicknamed Erik the Red, founded a colony in Greenland.

Erik had settled in Iceland, having been forced out of Norway, reportedly "because of some killings." There he married and had a son, Leif. However, he found no peace in Iceland. Disputes between neighbours were violent, and eventually Erik was outlawed and banished once again. Recalling the story of Gunnbjorn's discovery of fifty years before, Erik decided to investigate the possibilities of a new settlement and sailed west, probably sometime around 985.

During the three years of his exile, Erik discovered a land very different from both Norway and Iceland, with their towering peaks and forbidding glaciers. On his return to Iceland, he took the explorer's privilege of naming the new land, and chose the name Greenland because, according to his saga, "he argued that men would be all the more drawn to go there if the land had an attractive name." However, this is perhaps being a little unfair to Erik, and certainly Greenland was not all ice and snow. In the late tenth century, the climate

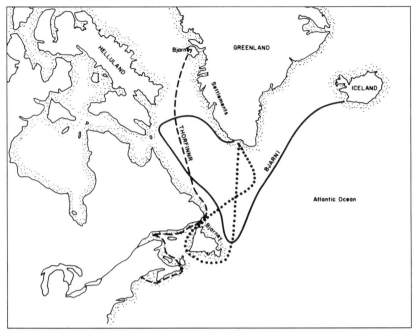

*An outline of the possible routes taken by Thorfinn Karlsefni and Bjarni Herjulfsson on their voyages west of Iceland.* (Drawing by Terry Dyer)

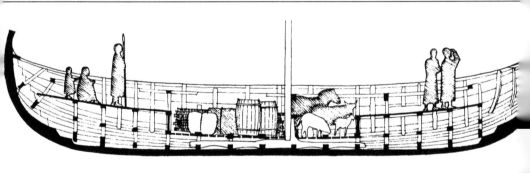

*Sketch of a Viking* knorr, *the ship favoured for trade and settlement. Although slower than the dragon ships used in raids on Europe, the* knorrs *were seaworthy and could carry a large volume of goods.* (Courtesy Viking Ship Museum, Roskilde, Denmark)

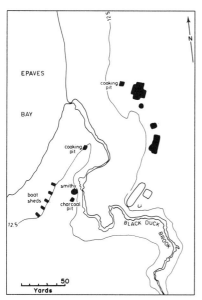

Plan of the Norse site at L'Anse aux Meadows showing the various houses, boat sheds, and associated cooking and working areas. (Courtesy *Canadian Geographic*)

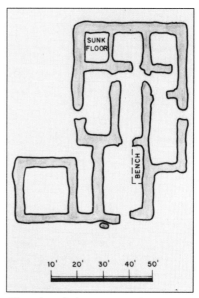

Floor plan of a house excavated at Brattahlid, at the head of a fjord in the eastern settlement. (Drawing by Terry Dyer)

*Norse dragon ship.* (Courtesy Trustees of the British Museum)

was considerably more temperate than in modern times. Pastureland at the head of the fjords was suitable for farming. The new land also offered an abundance of wildlife—bears, caribou, walrus and seals. The opportunities Erik described obviously sounded attractive, and when he returned, he led a fleet of more than twenty ships carrying potential settlers. The voyage was not easy and only fourteen ships arrived safely; the others were lost in bad weather or forced to turn back. The first settlers had the pick of the prime land; Erik chose the best site for himself and set up his farm at a place called Brattahlid (meaning "steep meadow"), which remained the homestead of the colony's leader for the next five hundred years. Farms were set up in two settlements: the eastern settlement, which was actually along the south coast, had about five thousand colonists, while the more northerly location—the western settlement—had about one thousand inhabitants.

No villages or towns were set up, either in Iceland or Greenland. Instead, the settlers lived in farmsteads located around the inner protected parts of the fjords, separated from each other by one to five kilometres. Generally, their farms were small, with only about ten to fifteen sturdy cattle, perhaps a hundred sheep and a few goats, although a few larger establishments could support at least twice as much livestock. The winters were long and cold and it was impossible to keep animals in the fields throughout the year. More food was required than could be provided by livestock farming alone, and the farmers augmented their diet by hunting caribou and seal. Caribou were taken as they migrated between winter and summer grazing grounds. Fortuitously, seals appeared off the coast in the spring, just as the long winter was ending and provisions were running out. Walrus and polar bear were also hunted, but much farther north, in an area known as the Nordsetar, probably just north of the Arctic Circle. The hunting of these animals was important for establishing trade links with Europe, because iron and wood, which were in short supply in Greenland, and grain, necessary for bread and other staples, had to be imported and could be exchanged for bear furs and ivory. The settlers produced no luxury goods, so these also had to come from Europe.

Christianity came early to the colony. Erik's wife was Christian, although he was not, and the first priest was brought by his son, Leif. He and his mother were both buried in the church built near their farm, and their bones, excavated in 1967, now lie in Copenhagen. By 1127 the colony was well enough established to bring in a bishop. The colony flourished for more than a century, when it came under the influence of Norway, which had taken over Iceland between 1261 and 1264. From that time on, things began to go wrong. Norway was just entering a period of decline and its rulers could do little to help their neighbours in Iceland, not to mention the more remote colonies in Greenland. In addition, the climate deteriorated significantly in the thirteenth and fourteenth centuries. Winters became longer and more severe, and fewer cattle survived in the dark fetid byres. Young calves were born indoors, sickly or stillborn, and the seal migration was disrupted by worsening ice conditions.

Bad ice conditions hampered trade with Europe, and this sounded the colony's death knell. The Greenlanders learned little from the Eskimos, who were much better adapted to the cold, harsh environment. Instead, they made every attempt to maintain their traditional way of life which, in the end, was a costly mistake. The strong family, church and trade links with Europe sustained the colony for almost five hundred years, but without these connections the Greenland colony was just not viable. Cut off from friends and family, and beset by ever colder winters and shorter summers, the colony began to collapse. By 1350 the western settlement was extinct, and by 1500 the last of the Vikings had died. Long before this, however, some colonists crossed the Davis Strait to the North American continent.

From the west coast of Greenland, the distance to Baffin Island is less than four hundred kilometres at its nearest point. It would have been surprising if such intrepid voyagers had not made this short crossing, although it was in fact accident that brought Bjarni Herjolfsson across. Sailing from Iceland to Greenland in 986, he was blown south and west past Cape Farewell at the southern tip of Greenland. The "following wind died down and north winds and fog overtook them, so that they had no idea of where they were going." Eventually, however, the fog lifted, and after another day's sailing, they saw land "covered in forest, with low hills." This was certainly not Greenland. Bjarni did not go ashore but sailed north, seeing first some very flat land, and then three days farther on, high rocky mountains. Turning east, he got back on track and arrived four days later in Greenland. His discovery was eagerly discussed in the colony, with the result that Leif, Erik's son, bought Bjarni's ship and set off to retrace his route with a crew of thirty-five.

Sailing west, Leif came to the same mountainous rocky coast. Going ashore "they could see no grass there. The background was all great glaciers and right up to the glaciers from the sea as if it were a single slab of rock." The land looked barren, and he named it Helluland, "land of flat rocks," which has been clearly identified as Baffin Island to the north of Hudson Strait. Three days' sailing south—the time it took Bjarni to sail north—brought Leif to the thickly forested shores of Labrador, which he named Markland, land of trees. Two days farther south Leif came to a place where "they had never known anything as sweet" as the dew on the grass, where there "was no lack of salmon ... in rivers or lakes. The land was so choice ... no frost came during the winter, and the grass was hardly withered. Day and night were of a more equal length there than in Greenland and Iceland. On the shortest day of winter the sun was visible in the middle of the afternoon as well as at breakfast time." Leif and his companions decided to spend the winter in this paradise, to have time to explore. The sailing season in Greenland waters was short, probably only from the end of June to October, so they would have had little time to spend there if they had returned home before winter set in. During an exploratory foray, one of the company found vines and grapes, so Leif named the place Vinland—land of the wine.

Early the next year, Leif and his crew returned to Greenland, their ship laden with lumber and grapes, probably now in the form of raisins or wine. Finding that his father had died during his absence, Leif remained in Greenland as leader of the settlements. His brother, Thorvald, however, continued the exploration of Vinland, returning to Leifsbudir, the camp set up by Leif, to spend the winter.

In the spring, on a journey west, they made contact with native inhabitants, whom they called "Skraelings." The meaning of this name is not clear: it may be the "ugly ones" or perhaps the "screechers" or simply the "savages." Nor is it certain whether they were Inuit or Indians. Thorvald discovered a group of them hiding under a canoe and killed all but one who escaped and returned later bent on revenge. That night the Vikings were attacked by a large group of Skraelings armed with spears and arrows. Thorvald's men managed to beat off, but Thorvald himself was killed by an arrow. He was quickly buried, and the party sailed home without him. Erik the Red's third son, Thorstein, promptly set off in 1007, apparently to find and bring back the body of his brother. However, bad fogs and contrary winds forced him back to Greenland without ever finding Leifsbudir. Thorvald, therefore, is the first European known to be buried in North America.

These setbacks delayed further expeditions to Vinland until about 1020, when Thorfinn Karlsefni, who had married the widow of Thorstein, decided to attempt the journey. It seems that this time, however, the intention was to put down roots and establish a permanent settlement. Their first winter was spent in great hardship, but during the second year they moved south and settled in an area with good pastureland and a milder climate. Once again the Skraelings appeared, but this time the contacts were of a peaceful nature. The natives arrived suddenly, stayed briefly and left. The next year they reappeared and, to the surprise of the Vikings, brought with them "furs and sables and skins of all kind," as if well aware of the Norsemen's wish to trade, and knowledgeable about what goods would be acceptable. This might indicate that the natives had earlier contact with Europeans for trading purposes. For instance, it has long been speculated that the Irish "papar," who disappeared from Iceland after the Norse arrived, had moved west and had eventually finished up on the shores of North America. The fact that the Skraelings were ready to trade, and had the furs which the Norse wanted, without any prompting is not the only reason for this supposition, however. During his stay in the area, Thorfinn captured two Indian boys near the coast. They were taught to speak some Norse and eventually learned enough to describe their country to the Norsemen. Of particular interest to Thorfinn was their account of "a country that lay on the other side, opposite their own land, where men walked about in white clothes and shouted loudly and carried poles and went about with flags." They concluded that this must be Hvritamannaland or "Ireland the great." Irish monks did wear white habits, and the processions described by the boys seem more reminiscent of a church ritual than of Indian or Inuit gatherings.

Peaceful relations between the two peoples did not last long. The Skraelings were happy to obtain woven cloth for the skins they had to trade, and were content even when the amount of cloth, which was running in short supply, had decreased to only about a finger's width for each skin. Soon, however their interest turned to weapons, which Thorfinn would not allow. Before long, it was necessary to erect a defensive pallisade around the camp, and not long after its construction, they were under attack. Although steel weapons were superior to those made from stone, the Vikings were not able to overcome their attackers. Thorfinn's difficulties were compounded by arguments and squabbling which broke out within the encampment, and after three winters, it was obvious that they could not hold out much longer. With this realization, they turned their backs on the settlement and returned to Greenland. These efforts, which began around 1000 AD, did not result in any permanent settlement, but the knowledge was not lost. Periodic voyages to Vinland followed Thorfinn's return, and although they were few and far between, there are references to a Vinland connection as late as the fourteenth century.

Although Markland and Helluland have been fairly well identified, there is still considerable controversy over the location of Vinland. Those who believed the descriptions in the sagas maintained that the land of wine must be well to the south. However, Vinland was said to be only four days' sail south of Markland, and certainly vines could not grow at that latitude if Markland was correctly identified as the coast of Labrador. For some years it was thought that Vinland would be more correctly translated as meadow or pastureland, but modern scholars are now mainly of the opinion that "Vin" does, indeed, relate to grapes or vines. The problems of location were until fairly recently compounded by Viking remains and artifacts found along the eastern seaboard, from Maine south to Cape Cod. However, with one exception, a Viking coin which was minted long after the

Vinland voyages, all of these remains and artifacts have been shown to be of doubtful origin—either hoaxes or attributable to some other culture. Only one site in North America has been proved beyond any doubt to be Viking and to have been occupied around 1000 AD—the site at L'Anse aux Meadows, at the top of the Northern Peninsula of Newfoundland.

The Viking presence at L'Anse aux Meadows was established in 1960 by the Norwegian lawyer and writer Helge Ingstad. Careful excavation since then has shown a typical Viking settlement with three large sod houses, each adjacent to a small dwelling which may have been used for slaves. The settlement stands about one hundred metres from the shoreline, located on a narrow terrace beside a peat bog. A forge was found nearby, and a smithy and carpenter's shop have been identified. The site has been dated, partly using radiocarbon techniques and partly from the style of the buildings and artifacts, to indicate a date within about five years of 1000 AD.

The sod houses were heated with long, narrow central fireplaces which were also used for cooking and light during the long winter nights. Excavation revealed artifacts similar to those found in houses of the same age in Greenland and Iceland. A bronze cloak pin was found in the cooking pit of one of the large dwellings, and a stone oil lamp was discovered in another building. Knitting needles and spindle whorls show that women were present, and there may also have been children. Local bog iron was smelted and forged on the site, providing nails and rivets, and there is evidence from woodworking debris that logs and planks had been trimmed and smoothed with metal tools.

From studies of the slag found around the smithy, it has been deduced that only a small quantity of iron, perhaps as little as 2.5 kilograms, was produced. Most of the iron would have gone into the manufacture of nails, and this, together with the evidence of woodworking, suggests that the major purpose of the work was to repair and service ships. Iron nails were not used in house construction, only in boat-building, and as they rusted quickly in saltwater, the boats were in frequent need of repair.

Unlike the scattered homesteads of Iceland and Greenland, L'Anse aux Meadows contains three full dwelling complexes in very close proximity. No barns or cattle sheds have been discovered despite extensive archaeological investigation, and it is clear that the settlement was never intended for farming. Instead, it looks most similar to the arrangements set up at various trading centres where ships could land to load trade goods. These centres included dwelling houses, storage areas, and workshops that were often linked to facilities for repairing ships. However, the L'Anse aux Meadows site was not used for trading. Excavation in the middens shows that it was occupied for only a few years, probably as a base for exploration. The sod houses were capable of accommodating about one hundred people without overcrowding and would have provided a safe camp for overwintering while the ships were being repaired for the long and hazardous journey back to Greenland.

There is no way to tell whether this is where Leif set up his first camp in America. Certainly it is the right distance south from Markland, but equally certainly, it is too far north for wild vines to flourish. However, a few butternuts were found at L'Anse aux Meadows. These are not native to the area and are too large to have been brought in by birds and too heavy to have floated in by sea. Logic suggests that they were brought to L'Anse aux Meadows by men. Butternuts have a northern limit around New Brunswick—about the same limit as wild grapes, so it appears that the Norse travelled south to where these plants could be found. At that time, the land on the southern shore of the Gulf of St. Lawrence was home to several Indian tribes, but the area around L'Anse aux Meadows was relatively unpopulated. Perhaps the Vikings travelled south from L'Anse aux Meadows to the southern shore of the Gulf of St. Lawrence, the home of a number of Indian tribes. L'Anse aux Meadows was a safe staging post at the very edge of Vinland, lying about a day's journey to the south. At the very least, it is indisputable proof of a Viking presence in North America four hundred years before Columbus.

# CHAPTER THREE

# *JOHN CABOT AND THE MEN OF BRISTOL*

*I*t is not evident what knowledge was passed on to later adventurers about Viking exploration of the New World. Folk memories do not die easily, and even without the written evidence of the sagas, the idea of "land to the west" persisted for a considerable time, so that by the end of the fifteenth century, Europeans were beginning to ponder the potential of the Atlantic Ocean. Portuguese and English merchants, in particular, were moving west in exploratory journeys. Maps of the time showed imaginary islands—Brasil, St. Brendan's Isle, Antilla and the like. These, together with the Portuguese discovery of the Azores, Canaries and Cape Verde Islands between 1431 and 1460, stimulated westward voyages.

England, in the meantime, had been looking north for quite different reasons. In the early fifteenth century, English fishermen had found plentiful supplies of cod in the waters around Iceland. Before long, the fishermen were followed by Bristol merchants, and a brisk trade in Icelandic products was soon established. At that time, the colony in Greenland was still in existence, but only just surviving. Fifteenth-century European artifacts found in Greenland graves attest to continued contact until then, but the links were very tenuous. As time passed, exports from Greenland ceased to have much importance. Royal ships stopped sailing on a regular basis, and the last bishop appointed by Rome sailed out in 1386. By 1470, the Danish king, Christian I, was so uncertain of the state of his westerly province that he sent out two ships to renew contact. No records exist of their return or of any further contact after that date.

With English fishermen working the Icelandic waters near the beginning of the century, it is probable that some knowledge of the presence and general location of Greenland would have become available over the years. Whether this information extended to the Markland or Vinland discoveries is unknown and not likely to be clarified. However, it seems likely that some knowledge would be transferred, considering that English fishermen were in contact with Iceland at the beginning of the century, and that knowledge of the colony was still current, at least in court circles, towards the end of the century. The colony itself is thought to have survived until some time between the middle of the fifteenth and the beginning of the sixteenth century.

Bristol merchants not only followed the fishermen north, however. They also sailed southwest to trade in the newly discovered Atlantic islands, beginning as early as 1480 in Madeira and possibly in the Azores and the Canary Islands. The Portuguese discoveries of these islands provided a general stimulation to exploration, especially to the experienced Atlantic navigators from Bristol looking for other trading opportunities.

In the latter part of the fifteenth century it was common for a group of merchants to share the costs of an expedition. They obtained less profit from successful voyages, but they shared the risk of little or no financial return. It was probably a group of Bristol merchants who commissioned a ship of eighty tons, commanded by John Lloyd, to search for the island of Brasil. This legendary island is shown in later medieval maps as a small, idealized island, circular or half-moon in shape, and lying not far off the coast of Ireland. The Bristolians, however, were convinced that the island lay much farther to the west, and John Lloyd spent nine weeks looking for it. Despite lack of success in 1480, the Bristol merchants persevered, and in the following year, another two ships, the *George* and the *Trinity*, were equipped to search for Brasil. Little is known of the voyage, except that it too was unsuccessful.

No records exist of additional expeditions in the years immediately following 1481, but in 1498 a Spanish representative in London wrote to King Ferdinard and Queen Isabella telling them that "for the last seven years the people of Bristol have equipped two, three [and] four caravels to go in search of the island of Brasil and the Seven Cities."[1] According to this report, voyages were made almost every year in the early 1490s, although no formal reports exist. There are indirect suggestions, however, that the Bristol adventurers found Newfoundland and kept very quiet about their discovery. There certainly might have been some financial advantage from not announcing the discovery of new fishing grounds, but it is difficult to imagine that anyone discovering a large piece of land so far west of England would not seek to obtain the glory of discovery, together with the possibility of immense profits if the King could be persuaded to grant a restricted trading licence.

Nevertheless, there are several separate pieces of evidence that suggest that this may indeed have happened. The first, but least convincing, lies in the notation of the Paris map printed in 1544, which is lodged in the Bibliothèque Nationale in Paris.[2] Near Cape Breton are written the words, "this land was discovered by John Cabot, the Venetian, and Sebastian Cabot his son, in the year of the birth of our Saviour Jesus Christ 1494 on the 24th of June in the morning to which they gave the name Land First Seen and to a large island near the said land they gave the name Saint John because it had been discovered on the same day." Cabot, a Venetian, who sailed on behalf of Bristol merchants, publicized his discovery of the "New Founde Lande" three years later, and it must be assumed that the copyist (if indeed the Paris map is a copy of the original—other copies of the same era are known to exist) made a mistake and entered 1494 instead of 1497. Cabot himself claimed that his 1497 voyage was the one in which he made the discovery, and all the other sources suggest that the writing on the Paris map is a simple error. Nevertheless, the date is intriguing and fits with other, much more convincing evidence to suggest that the Bristol merchants made their discovery before Cabot's famous voyage in 1497.

In 1957 a letter was discovered in the Spanish Archives that described some aspects of the 1497 voyage of John Cabot.[3] Written by an English merchant named John Day, resident in Spain at the time of writing (probably around December 1497 or early the following year), it was addressed to the Lord Grand Admiral, presumed to be Columbus. Day's letter is obviously written in reply to a letter received from Columbus in which he seems to have requested information on the geography of the mainland and islands in the area Cabot visited. Day describes Cabot's voyage of 1497 and his plan to return in 1498 with more ships, but towards the end of his narrative he adds a brief aside, saying, "It is considered certain that the cape of the said land was found and discovered in the past by the men from Bristol who found 'Brasil' as your Lordship well knows. It was called the Island of Brasil and it is assumed and believed to be the mainland that the men of Brasil found." This states quite clearly that the "men from Bristol" discovered land in the north prior to Cabot's first successful voyage in 1497. Day does not give any dates or say who exactly made the discovery but these can perhaps be deduced from other sources.

Almost thirty years after Cabot's voyage, an Englishman, Robert Thorne, writing from Seville to the English ambassador to Spain, presents an idea for a voyage of exploration. In explaining his motives, Thorne describes how his desire was "inherited of my Father which with an[other] Merchant of Brystow named Hugh Elliot [were] the discoverers of the Newfoundlande."[4] Thorne gives no date for this discovery, and the word does not necessarily imply that his father, also Robert Thorne, was the first Englishman to see Newfoundland. "Discoverers" could mean only that Thorne had made Cabot's discovery clearer by uncovering the secrets of the new land. Alternatively, Thorne and Elliot could have sailed with Cabot in 1497, but there is no way of confirming this. The original letter has long since disappeared. It is interesting to note, however, that contemporary writers who had access to the original did not consider either of these two possibilities. Dr. Dee, Queen Elizabeth's geographer and necromancer, wrote a justification of England's possession of North America around 1577. At that time, he had Thorne's unpublished letter in his possession, and while correctly giving 1497 as the date of Cabot's discovery, he puts Thorne and Elliot's expedition down to 1494, the date attributed to Cabot on the Paris map. Dee may have had other evidence, perhaps marginal comments on the original letter that did not survive on the copies, but we cannot be sure. There is a possibility of a discovery in 1494, but no certainty.

English knowledge of the North Atlantic in the 1490s had been gathered by Bristol merchants trading actively with Iceland and the Atlantic islands farther south, some of them like the Azores, being almost a thousand miles out from Spain. They were looking for the island of Brasil and may well have found it (Newfoundland) lying close to the shores of mainland North America. With this interest and activity, it is difficult at first to understand why Columbus's request for support for a westward voyage was not supported by King Henry VII. However, when Columbus's brother Bartholomew arrived in London in 1488-89 bearing the request, Henry had other things on his mind. At that time England was far from the great power she would become in his granddaughter's day. The country was small and poor and had an exceedingly small population relative to the major European powers. Numbers are difficult to estimate, but the best guesses indicate a total population of around 2 million in 1400, rising by only about half a million in the next hundred years. As late as 1520 the population of the largest city, London, was only about 60,000, compared, for example, with 230,000 in Naples and nearly 200,000 in Paris. In this situation England was relatively unimportant in European circles. What is perhaps more important, she had been tearing herself apart in the War of the Roses until 1485, and was just settling down to peace and stability. Henry had won the crown by force of arms. His dynasty was new, and there were others in England with an equally good claim to the throne. This was hardly a time to be encouraging foreign ventures, and Bartholomew was turned away. Columbus, of course, eventually received his support from Spain, which benefited greatly by supporting him.

There can be little doubt that news of Columbus's success in 1492 influenced the King's decision when he received another proposal (similar to the one he had refused) from John Cabot in 1496. This time he did not hesitate to issue letters of patent giving "full and free authority, faculty and power to sail to all parts, regions and coasts of the eastern, western and northern sea, under our banners, flags and ensigns, with five ships or vessels of whatsoever burden and quality they may be, and with so many and with such mariners and men as they may wish to take with them in the said ships, at their own proper costs and charges, to find, discover and investigate whatsoever islands, countries, regions or provinces of heathens and infidels, in whatsoever part of the world placed, which before this time were unknown to all Christians."[5]

To allow some profit for Cabot and his sons, Henry VII also decreed, as was quite usual, that none of his other subjects could visit any of the "mainlands, islands, towns, cities, castles and other places whatsoever discovered by them" unless they had first acquired a licence, and presumably paid for it, from "the aforesaid John and his sons and ... deputies." They were also to be free of all customs duties but were to pay to the King one-fifth of their profits.

Who then was this "well beloved John Cabot, Citizen of Venice," and how did he come to be in London petitioning the King with grandiose schemes for discovery in the North Atlantic? Surprisingly, considering his place among the first Europeans to set foot in the New World, there is remarkably little known about his origins. He is first mentioned in historical records between 1471 and 1473, when he was granted citizenship of Venice. The grant was confirmed on March 29, 1476, stating that it was made under the usual condition that he had "already inhabited Venice continuously for years," which suggests that he had resided there primarily since at least 1451.[6] Prior to this, there is some evidence to show that he had been a citizen of Genoa, being later described after returning from a successful voyage as "another Genoese like Columbus."[7] There is absolutely no information about his date of birth, nor are there any contemporary portraits. Indeed, this shadowy character was so little known that from the middle of the sixteenth century to the end of the nineteenth, historians generally attributed his exploits to Sebastian Cabot, his son, who did nothing during his lifetime (he died in 1557) to correct this mistaken impression. It is known that Cabot was a merchant, that he had, on previous occasions, been to Mecca in pursuit of the spice trade, and that he had conducted many conversations with the caravan drivers regarding the source of their precious cargo. He was also familiar with

Marco Polo's book, which was, at that time, largely unknown in England.

Cabot's reasons for leaving Venice and coming to England are quite unknown. He may have realized that England was at the far end of the spice route and that English merchants might therefore have most to gain from a short westerly sea route to Cathay. He may have heard of the exploits of the Bristol adventurers and of their efforts to find Brasil. Almost certainly he did not believe that Columbus had discovered the fabled lands of the Great Khan, and there are intriguing records to suggest that he may have gone to Lisbon and Seville before taking his project to Henry VII of England. Alternatively, he may just have decided that England, lying to the north of continental Europe, was the best jumping-off point for a trip northwest to Cathay. By 1495 he had moved to England and was in Bristol finding funds for just such a voyage. Unlike Columbus, however, this one would strike a route north and west.

The Bristol merchants gave Cabot their whole-hearted support. Prior to his arrival in England, their exploratory ventures had concentrated almost entirely on the mythical island of Brasil, and the merchants had no thoughts of Cathay. This changed, however, when Cabot approached them only a few years after knowledge of Columbus's discoveries had circulated through the civilized world. With his experience of other lands and his knowledge of Marco Polo's Cipangu and Cathay, Cabot must have sparked the enthusiasm of these fifteenth-century entrepreneurs. They enthusiastically switched their interest from Atlantic islands to Cabot's dream of a westerly route to the East.

With their plans drawn up and complete, Cabot and his backers approached the King, probably late in 1495, and the letters of patent were issued on March 5, 1496. These specifically excluded exploration in the southern Atlantic, south of the latitude of England. Henry VII was prepared to recognize Spain's claim to the land discovered by Columbus, but he certainly did not intend to submit meekly to the provisions of the Papal treaty of Tordesillas, which had carved up the globe between Portugal and Spain. Having missed the opportunity offered by Columbus, the King of England did not intend to let the

*Title page of a Tudor nautical manual giving "the courfes, heights, diftances, depths and foundings, flouds and ebs, rifings of lands, rocks, fands and fhoalds, with the marks for th'entrings of the Harbouroughs, Havens and Ports of the greateft part of Europe."* (Courtesy British Library)

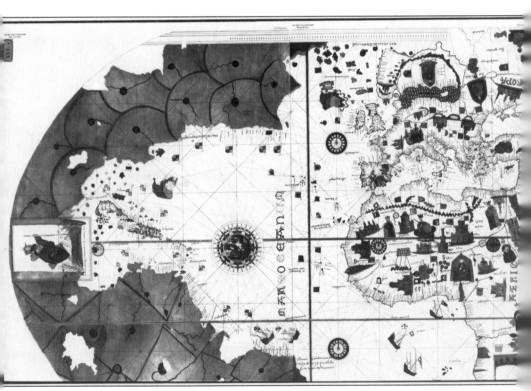

*World map drawn by Juan de la Cosa in 1500 showing the North American coastline and the West Indies. De la Cosa sailed with Columbus and made three other voyages to America. Facsimile from Jomard's* Monuments de la Geographie ... *(Paris, 1842-62).* (Courtesy National Archives of Canada, NMC 10030)

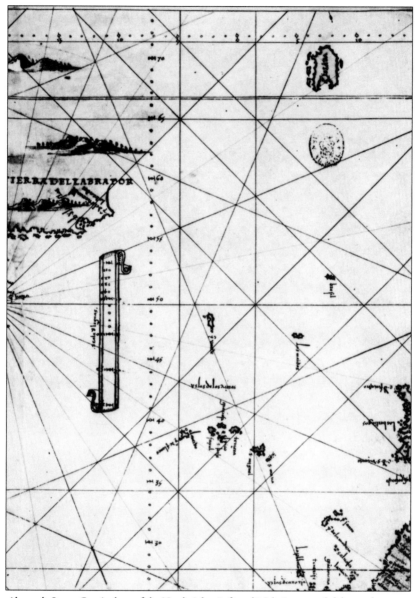

*Alonso de Santa Cruz's chart of the North Atlantic from his* Islario general del mundo *(1545). The map still shows the imaginary islands of Brasil, Las Maidas, and the Green Island* (ya verde) *in the middle of the ocean.* (Courtesy Biblioteca Naçional, Madrid)

IMAGINARY MEDALLION PORTRAIT
OF JOHN CABOT.

By Carlo Barrera Pezzi. From
a memoir published in Venice in 1881.

*An imaginary portrait of John Cabot by C.B. Pezzi, 1881.*
(Courtesy National Archives of Canada)

*Shipbuilding techniques in Europe at the time of the great discoveries. To make planks, workers sawed trees along their length, with one standing above the tree, the other in a pit below ground level.* (Engraving by J. Sadeler. Courtesy National Maritime Museum, Greenwich)

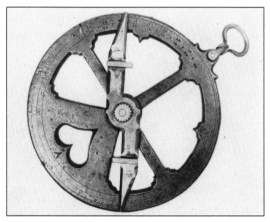

*A mariner's astrolobe, c. 1600. This instrument was developed by the Portuguese in the late fifteenth and early sixteenth centuries and was used to measure the angle of the sun relative to the horizon, a means of finding the ship's latitude.* (Courtesy Museum of the History of Science, Oxford and the Bettman Archives, New York)

whole of the New World slip through his fingers.

Cabot's voyage of 1497 is well documented, although his actual log was lost. Until recently it was thought that he had spent a whole year or so preparing for the voyage. However, the letter written by John Day to Columbus mentions an earlier voyage—presumably in 1496. Day's letter, the only evidence of this earlier expedition, says, "He went with one ship, he fell out with his crew, he was short of supplies and ran into bad weather and he decided to turn back."[8] Small wonder!

Following this initial setback, Cabot renewed his preparations, and probably towards the end of May, he sailed from Bristol in another small ship, the *Matthew*. Possibly named after Cabot's wife, Mattea, this one was fifty "tuns" in size, meaning it could carry fifty tuns of wine, She had a complement of twenty, which included two of Cabot's friends, some Bristol merchants and possibly Cabot's son Sebastian.

Their route took the small ship north and west across the Atlantic, probably following the route used by the Vikings. In common with other explorers of his day, he would most likely have picked a latitude between 50°N and 52°N. In the absence of his log, there is no assurance regarding his point of landfall, and for the last two hundred years there has been ongoing controversy over its exact location. From reports he made on his return to England, it seems clear that he sighted the mainland of North America on June 24, the feast of St. John the Baptist. He then sailed south for three hundred leagues, but where exactly he was is still a mystery. The best evidence seems to suggest a landfall in Labrador or northern Newfoundland, but he has also been placed at Cape Breton in Nova Scotia and as far south as Maine in the United States.

He landed briefly, taking possession of the land for the King. He made no contact with the inhabitants but was quite sure that the land was inhabited. In his letter to Columbus, John Day recounts how "they found a trail that went inland, they saw a site where a fire had been made, they saw manure of animals which they thought to be farm animals, and they saw a stick half a yard long pierced at both ends, carved and painted with brazil, and by such signs they believe the land to be inhabited."[9] Since there were only twenty people with him, he did not dare advance inland beyond the shooting distance of a crossbow, and after taking in fresh water, he returned to his ship. Assuming that he had discovered the outer regions of Cathay, Cabot set sail for England and arrived home in Bristol on August 6.

His arrival caused great excitement. News of the discovery spread quickly, and people ran after him in the streets hailing him as "the great admiral." Henry VII provided an immediate reward, "£10, to hym that founde the new Isle," and settled an annuity on him of £20 per year.[10] One of the four contemporary reports of his voyage is contained in a letter[11] written by the Milanese ambassador. The letter is dated December 18 and is worth quoting in its entirety:

> Perhaps amid the numerous occupations of your Excellency, it may not weary you to hear how his Majesty here has gained a part of Asia, without a stroke of the sword. There is in this Kingdom a man of the people, Messer Zoane Caboto by name, of kindly wit and a most expert mariner. Having observed that the sovereigns first of Portugal and then of Spain had occupied unknown islands, he decided to make a similar acquisition for his Majesty. After obtaining patents that the effective ownership of what he might find should be his, though reserving the rights of the Crown, he committed himself to fortune in a little ship, with eighteen persons. He started from Bristol, a port on the west of this kingdom, passed Ireland, which is still farther west, and then bore towards the north, in order to sail to the east, leaving the north on his right hand after some days. After having wandered for some time he at length arrived at the mainland, where he hoisted the royal standard, and took possession for the king here; and after taking certain tokens he returned.
>
> This Messer Zoane, as a foreigner and a poor man, would not have obtained credence, had it not been that his companions, who are practically all English and from Bristol, testified that he spoke the truth. This Messer Zoane has the description of the world in a map, and also in a solid sphere, which he has made, and shows where he has

been. In going towards the east he passed far beyond the country of the Tanais. They say that the land is excellent and temperate, and they believe that Brazil wood and silk are native there. They assert that the sea there is swarming with fish, which can be taken not only with the net, but in baskets let down with a stone, so that it sinks in the water. I have heard this Messer Zoane state so much.

These same English, his companions, say that they could bring so many fish that this kingdom would have no further need of Iceland, from which place there comes a very great quantity of the fish called stockfish. But Messer Zoane has his mind set upon even greater things, because he proposes to keep along the coast from the place at which he touched, more and more towards the east, until he reaches an island which he calls Cipango, situated in the equinoctial region, where he believes that all the spices of the world have their origin, as well as the jewels. He says that on previous occasions he has been to Mecca, whither spices are borne by caravans from distant countries. When he asked those who brought them what was the place of origin of these spices, they answered that they did not know, but that other caravans came with this merchandise to their homes from distant countries, and these again said that the goods had been brought to them from other remote regions. He therefore reasons that these things come from places far away from them, and so on from one to the other, always assuming that the earth is round, it follows as a matter of course that the last of all must take them in the north towards the west.

He tells all this in such a way, and makes everything so plain, that I also feel compelled to believe him. What is much more, his Majesty, who is wise and not prodigal, also gives him some credence, because he is giving him a fairly good provision, since his return, so Messer Zoane himself tells me. Before very long they say that his Majesty will equip some ships, and in addition he will give them all the malefactors, and they will go to that country and form a colony. By means of this they hope to make London a more important mart for spices than Alexandria. The leading men in this enterprise are from Bristol, and great seamen, and now they know where to go, say that the voyage will not take more than a fortnight, if they have good fortune after leaving Ireland.

I have also spoken with a Burgundian, one of Messer Zoane's companions, who corroborates everything. He wants to go back, because the Admiral, which is the name they give to Messer Zoane, has given him an island. He has given another to his barber, a Genoese by birth, and both consider themselves counts, while my lord the Admiral esteems himself at least a prince. I also believe that some poor Italian friars will go on this voyage, who have the promise of bishoprics. As I have made friends with the Admiral, I might have an archbishopric if I chose to go there, but I have reflected that the benefices which your Excellency reserves for me are safer, and I therefore beg that possession may be given me of those which fall vacant in my absence, and the necessary steps taken so that they may not be taken away from me by others who have the advantage of being on the spot. Meanwhile I stay on in this country, eating ten or twelve courses at each meal, and spending three hours at table twice every day, for the love of your Excellency, to whom I humbly commend myself.

Cabot quickly planned a fully equipped trading venture for the following year, 1498. Eventually five ships were outfitted—one of which King Henry VII contributed—and the merchants of London and Bristol put the cargoes together, some with the aid of loans from the Crown. A colony was considered for which, the King promised, convicts would be conscripted to undertake the necessary hard labour.

This second expedition set out in May 1498, again from Bristol. One of the five ships was damaged in a violent storm soon after they left, and put into an Irish port. The other four sailed on into oblivion, and it is not known what became of them. It has been speculated that Cabot did again achieve a landfall in North America. Some European artifacts were later found among natives in the area of Newfoundland, and this has been taken as reasonable evidence of some contact during the second voyage. Records show that at least one member of this expedition returned to England and was alive in London in 1501, but he may well have been on the damaged ship which never attempted the crossing. Cabot's annuity was paid until September 1499, but this is by no means proof that he was alive to collect it. The money may well have been paid to his wife only for as long as the government had no proof that he was dead. Later Spanish concerns over English influence to the north have also been taken to indicate that Cabot not only reached the mainland but sailed sufficiently far south to interfere with Spanish interests. In a Spanish patent of 1501, the recipient, Alonso de Hojeda, was encouraged to make his way to the vicinity of Venezuela, where he had apparently made some earlier discoveries, and then to proceed north, "where it has been learnt that the English were making discoveries; and that you go setting up markers with the arms of their Majesties, or with other signs that may be known ... in order that it be known that you have discovered this land, so that you may stop the exploration of the English in that direction."[12]

If the English did stop, it was only for a short while, waiting perhaps for the return of Cabot and his four ships. Nevertheless, the pause of a few years was sufficient for the Portuguese from the Azores to fill the gap. In 1500 a nobleman, Gaspar Corte Réal, sailed northwest and rediscovered Greenland, largely lost to European knowledge by that time. News of his discovery was brought to England in the following year by Juan (or Jaoa) Fernandez, also from the Azores. Fernandez was a small landowner in the Azores, known as a "llabrador," and because of this, Greenland became known as the "land of the Labrador," the name only being transferred to its current location in northeast Canada at a later date. Gaspar Corte Réal undertook another voyage in 1501. Two of his three ships were sent home after reaching the coast of North America. Corte Réal pressed on in the third and disappeared. His brother, Miguel, set out in 1502—at least partly in search of Gaspar—and he too was lost.

By this time it must have been fairly apparent that Cabot had been no more successful than Columbus in discovering the lands of Cathay. Rather than being the outlying parts of the Great Khan's territory, the new land to the west had become a barrier, and these voyages were most probably an early attempt to find a passage through the northwest.

In England during this time, Juan Fernandez, the "llabrador," had joined forces with various others in Bristol. Letters of patent were issued to him and his colleagues (two other Portuguese and three Bristol merchants) in 1501, the same year as Gaspar's first sailing. Two voyages in successive years may be recognized from grants paid by the King in January and September of 1502 to the "merchantes of bristoll that have bene in the newe founde lande."[13] A special pension of £10 a year was given to Fernandez and one of his Azorean colleagues "in consideracion of the true service which they have doon unto us to oure singular pleasure as Capitaignes into the newe founde lande." These grants suggest voyages from Bristol in 1501 and the early part of 1502. In the second, three natives were kidnapped and brought back to England. "These were clothed in beastes skinnes, and ate rawe fleshe, and spake such speech that no man coulde understand them, and in their demeanour like to bruite beastes, whom the king kept a time after. Of the which upon two yeeres past after I saw two apparelled after the manner of Englishmen, in Westminister pallace, which at that time I coulde not discern from Englishmen, till I learned what they were. But as for speech, I heard none of them utter one worde."[14]

In 1502 a new patent was issued to overcome the constraints set on the English by the Corte Réal voyages. Prior to that time Henry VII had always issued patents which limited discovery and possession to lands not known to Christians. After the Corte Réal expeditions, these were of little use, as the Portuguese then had full knowledge of the existence of land to the north. Now, to circumvent his problems, Henry issued much more sweeping powers—powers which would indeed become the blueprint for the later British colonial empire. Fernandez and his backers were now authorized to "find, recover, discover and search out any islands, countries, regions or provinces whatsoever of heathens or infidels in whatsoever part of the world placed ... provided always that they in no wise occupy themselves with nor enter the lands, countries or provinces ... first discovered by the subject of our very dear brother and cousin the King of Portugal or by the subjects of any other princes soever, our friends and confederates and in possesson of which these same princes now find themselves."[15] These effectively permitted possession of any non-Christian lands which were not actively occupied by other European Powers. What Henry's "very dear brother and cousin" thought of this new development is not recorded.

Between 1503 and 1506, several voyages were made on this basis, and a group calling itself the "Company of Adventurers to the New Founde Lande" was established.[16] Voyages continued sporadically for the next twenty years. Sebastian Cabot, John's son, is thought to have led an expedition in 1508-1509 in search of a northwest passage. An abortive voyage, perhaps to Newfoundland, set out in 1517. Another effort to establish a presence in Newfoundland was made in 1521 under the direction of Cardinal Wolsey. Then in 1527 Henry VIII sent two ships to look for a passage to Asia by way of Davis Strait.

During these years, the Portuguese and Spanish were also sending ships to the Northwest, but just when French interest in Canada was beginning, the interest of the other European powers was declining. By 1534, the time of Cartier's first voyage, Portugal had established her eastern route to the Spice Islands and Spain was busy in the West Indies. England did not have alternative interests like these, but forty years of exploration with minimal return had exhausted her patience. The final abortive trip took place in 1536 under Captain Robert Hoare. Two ships sailed to Cape Breton and Newfoundland. Their food supply ran out, and after exhausting the possibilities of existing on bears and sea birds, the men resorted to cannibalism. Eventually they saved themselves by capturing a well-stocked French ship with which they made their way back to Bristol. This fiasco proved to be the final nail in the coffin of English exploration, and for the next fifty years English interests were directed to other spheres. The "new founde lande" was allowed to sink back into a fog of obscurity.

CHAPTER FOUR

# *T*HE FIRST FRENCH EXPEDITIONS

*F*ollowing Cabot's discovery of new lands to the west in 1497, France did little to emulate the Portuguese and English explorers. Not until 1523 did King Francis I begin to think it might be expedient to ensure that if riches could be gained by sailing north, France had better not be left out of the picture. By then, Francis had ample evidence of the gold that the Spanish were extracting from their colonies in South America. Western civilization was still ringing with the news of Magellan's recent circumnavigation of the globe, and the idea that there might be a passage north and west to Cathay and Cipangu was well known in the courts of Europe.

Eventually the French sent an expedition east to look for this route, headed by a Florentine, Giovanni da Verrazano, who sailed much farther south than the area explored by the Bristol merchants, and made a landfall along the coast of New Jersey. From there, after mistaking either Delaware or Chesapeake Bay for the Pacific, he turned north into New York harbour, explored Narragansett Bay in Rhode Island, and followed the coastline north to Maine. These tentative probings were followed in 1524-1525 by Estevan Gomez, who scouted the coasts from Nova Scotia to the Caribbean. His voyage made it fairly clear that Verrazano had not seen the Pacific, but there was still no indication of any passage through the land mass.

For almost ten years there was a lull in official French exploration, but this, as was the case in other countries, did not stop French fishermen from setting out in ever-increasing numbers for the rich fishery of the Grand Banks. Then in 1534, France tried again by financing a voyage which would ultimately bring great rewards.

57

Jacques Cartier, an experienced navigator of St. Malo, was commissioned to take two ships "to the New Lands to discover certain islands and countries where it is said that he should find great quantities of gold and other valuable things."[1] This was the official version but not necessarily the whole truth. In the early sixteenth century, the land mass of North America was still thought to be part of Asia, and Cartier's numerous references to his disappointment at not finding the passage suggest that he, at least, had undertaken the voyage primarily to look for such a passage through, or perhaps into, the interior. Although quite unsuccessful in his first voyage, his second expedition in 1535 opened up the St. Lawrence River and eventually, although with considerable delay, led to the founding of French Canada.

Little is known of the early life of Jacques Cartier. He was born in St. Malo in 1491 and was married, at the age of twenty-eight, to the daughter of the high constable. In the civil register he is described as a "master pilot of the port of Saincte-Malo,"[2] but there is no indication of how he rose to this rank. Almost certainly he was an experienced navigator and must have had knowledge of the Atlantic and the new islands which were being discovered. It is quite possible that at one time he had made the Atlantic crossing himself, and in his accounts of the three voyages he made to the Gulf of St. Lawrence after 1534, he compares the corn he found there with that "which groweth in Brezil."[3] Indeed, there is a suspicion that he may have brought a native Indian back with him from one of these voyages because in 1528 the baptismal register of St. Malo shows that his wife stood as godmother to a young child, or woman, named "Catherine of Brezil."[4] By the time he was chosen to head the French expedition in 1524, he was in his early forties, married for fifteen years but with no children.

With two small ships, each of about sixty tons burden, Cartier set sail from St. Malo on April 20, 1534. The full complement included only sixty-one men. Following the route opened up by fishermen, they sailed northwest towards Newfoundland and, with good winds and a fair crossing, arrived off the coast just three weeks after leaving port. This was a surprisingly fast crossing. In his third voyage, seven years and one month later, the weather was so bad it took a full three months to make the same voyage. However, in 1534 they arrived off Newfoundland when the pack ice was still close to the shore. Forced to turn south, Cartier anchored his ships in a harbour about 130 kilometres north of St. John's, where he sat out some bad weather and kept the men occupied in repairing the boats and getting them ready for the unknown seas ahead. After ten days they sailed north to Funk Island, where they replenished their supplies by killing so many sea birds—the now extinct great auk—that they filled two boats with them. Pressing on, they sailed up to the Strait of Belle Isle, headed west, and continued along the south shore of Labrador to the sands of Blanc Sablon and the harbour at Brest.

Cartier's exploration along the Labrador coastline showed no evidence of the "Edorado" he had come to seek. Instead, he remarked that it could hardly be considered "the new land but rather stones and wilde cragges and a place fit for wilde beastes." He had seen little or nothing of any worth. "In all the North Lland I did not see a Cart-load of good earth: yet when I went on shoare in many places, and in the Island of White Sand, there is nothing there but mosse and small thornes scattered here and there, withered and dry. To be short, I beleeve that this was the land that God allotted to Cain."

On June 15, they departed from Brest on a southerly course and sailed down the western side of the island of Newfoundland. This coast was also disappointing, but a change of course to the southwest on June 25 provided a pleasant surprise. First, they arrived at Bird Rock, northwest of the Magdalen Islands, where they again stocked up with sea birds. Cartier recorded that they killed and took away more than one thousand of them and swore that if it had been necessary, they could have filled thirty boatloads in an hour. A few leagues farther brought them to an island which they named Brion's Island in honour of the Seigneur de Brion, Admiral of France. This proved to be totally different to the harsh landscape of Labrador, and Cartier commented that one field of it was worth more than all the new land. They found it "full of goodly trees, medowes, fields full of wild corne and peason bloomed, as thick, as ranke, and as faire as any can be seene in Britaine, so that they seemed to have bene plowed and sowed. There was also a great store of gooseberies, strawberies, damaske roses, parseley with other sweete and pleasant hearbes." They saw a number of walruses which they described as "beastes as great as oxen which have two great teeth in their mouths like unto Elephant's teeth and live in the sea."

June 28 found them in the vicinity of the Magdalen Islands, and by July they were lying off the northern end of Prince Edward Island. From there they sailed over to the coast of New Brunswick and proceeded northwards past Miramichi Bay to find Chaleur Bay (Bay of Heat) opening up to the west. "The countrey," said Cartier, "is hotter than the countrey of Spain and the fairest that can possibly be found, altogether smooth and level." Again it was "full of wilde corne," and there were "white and red gooseberies, strawberies, blackberies, white and red Roses with many other floweres of very sweet and pleasant smell. There be also many goodly meadowes full of grasse, and lakes wherein great plentie of salmons be." Their hopes that this might provide a passage to the west were dashed on July 10 when, at about ten o'clock in the morning, they could see the head of the bay. Sailing back past the Gaspé Peninsula, they took a northeasterly course to run across the gulf to Anticosti Island.

Between July 27 and August 5 they sailed around the island, first along the southern shore, then round the eastern end and on up the northern coastline to within a few miles of the western point.

This was one of the most difficult parts of the voyage. Wind and tide were against them, and the ships made slow progress along the north coast of the island. They persevered, even lowering boats to attempt, in vain, to row into the wind. Cartier seems to have been fairly sure that this northern passage was worth pursuing. From the shores of Anticosti Island they could see the south coast of Quebec not too far away, and after landing on the island and taking a short march to the western end, they realized that there were open waters to the west. Unfortunately, the adverse weather prevented Cartier from pursuing this goal. By now, at the beginning of August, they had been away for three months, and it was getting late for further ventures into the unknown. After deliberating on the situation with his sailing masters and pilots, it was decided they should turn back. By August 9, with the wind behind them, they were back in Blanc Sablon. From there they passed again through the Strait of Belle Isle and, after some turbulent weather in mid-Atlantic, arrived safely home on September 5.

Cartier brought back little of immediate interest for King Francis. There was no gold or silver, no jewels, and no obvious route to the East. The land in the southern part of the Gulf of St. Lawrence was fertile and hospitable, with suitable trees for shipbuilding, but Francis was not interested in colonial ventures at that time, and his support of another voyage that left in 1535 was probably based on other considerations. By his careful navigation and charting, Cartier had shown that he was a highly competent navigator and that he might yet find a passage to the East among the bays and islands of the Gulf. In addition, there were other possibilities which seemed much more definite. During his first voyage Cartier had considerable contact with the natives. Only a few individuals had been seen on the shores of Labrador, but when he arrived at Chaleur Bay at the beginning of July, he had fallen in with a large group. Immediately after his arrival, Cartier anchored his two ships at Port Daniel, at the northern entrance to the bay, and explored the area with smaller boats. The ships remained there for about a week, during which time hundreds of Indians came and traded skins for knives and iron tools.

Later in the voyage, bad weather forced the expedition to remain anchored in Gaspé Bay for nine days, and again they met large numbers of Indians. The French considered them to be some of the poorest people they had ever seen, possessing nothing of value except their canoes and nets. Nevertheless, they found the Indians friendly, eager to examine the white skins and eager to barter. There was, however, reason for caution because very soon Cartier's men learned that they were also "very great theeves for they will filch and steale whatsoever they can lay hold of, and all is fish that commeth to net."

Before leaving Gaspé Bay, Cartier's men erected a large wooden cross and a shield bearing the fleur-de-lis emblem of France. But as soon as the French boarded their ships, the local chief appeared and made it clear, by way of sign language, that the land belonged to the Indians and not to the strangers. He was soon pacified, however, by additional gifts and by the explanation, also in sign language, that the cross had been erected only to mark the entrance to the bay. The chief and his followers were then persuaded to board one of the ships, where they were well entertained. Two young Indians were invited, and agreed to remain on board to travel back to France with Cartier. These men were not, however, from the Gaspé Peninsula but had come to the Gulf region on a summer expedition from Hochelaga. They were familiar with the St. Lawrence River as the route to Hochelaga, and also to two other Indian nations, Saguenay, which was downriver from Hochelaga, and Canada, in the interior.

Perhaps by the time Cartier's ships were blocked by the wind and tide in the passage between Anticosti Island and Quebec, and certainly before he began his second voyage, it must have become obvious to him that the St. Lawrence was a river, and not the much sought after northwest passage. Indeed, the Indians had described it as such, saying that it was the route to Canada, that it grew narrower as it approached Canada, that the water became fresh, and that it could only be navigated by small boats.

When he set sail on his second voyage in May 1535, Cartier was thus probably motivated more by the possibility of a route into the interior than by the possibility of finding another opening providing a passage to the East.

After the previous year's success, he was given command of a much larger expedition. Three ships were provided: the *Grande Hermine* of 120 tons, the *Petite Hermine* of 60 tons and a smaller ship, the *Emerillon,* of only 40 tons. These were outfitted with supplies sufficient to last for fifteen months, so that he might spend a winter in Canada, and carried a crew of 112 men, as well as the two Indians from the first voyage. They sailed on May 19, but after a good wind on leaving France, a storm blew up and separated the ships. Cartier arrived off Newfoundland on July 7 and proceeded up to Blanc Sablon, where he waited for the other ships at a rendezvous arranged before they left St. Malo. The others joined him there on July 26, and after a few days, they set out to explore. This time they were able to get through the passage between Quebec and Anticosti Island. The Indian guides then explained that the water ahead was the beginning of the river leading to Hochelaga and Canada. However, instead of heading immediately upstream, and perhaps with the hope of still finding a passage to Cathay, Cartier turned south and traversed the Gulf, bringing him again to the Gaspé Peninsula. From there, he circumnavigated the inner gulf until he arrived back at Sept Isles, on the northern shore, to explore the coast east towards Anticosti Island. Finding no open water, he then turned towards Hochelaga and sailed up the St. Lawrence as far as the Iroquois village called Stadacona, located near the site of today's Quebec City.

The Indians' initial fear at the sight of the three large ships was dispelled by Cartier's native guides, who spoke to them in their own language. Gifts were exchanged, and the Indians tried to persuade Cartier to stay at Stadacona instead of proceeding up the river. Over the next few days, every attempt was made to delay them, even to the extent of sending out a canoe with "three men like Divels being wrapped in dogges skinnes white and blacke, their faces besmeered as blacke as any coales, with hornes on their heads more then a yard long." According to the Indians, the "divels" had been sent by their great God Cudragny to warn Cartier that he must not attempt passage up the river because of the great dangers which would befall him. As might be expected, however, the French took little notice, and on September 19 they set out in the *Emerillon* accompanied by two longboats and fifty men. The two other ships and the rest of the company remained at Stadacona to erect a fort and prepare for the winter.

For two weeks they journeyed up the St. Lawrence, leaving the *Emerillon* when the river became too shallow and finishing the journey in the longboats with about two dozen men. As it was early September, Cartier was overwhelmed with the natural abundance of the land through which he passed. Timber was thick, wild nuts and fruits grew everywhere. One island off Stadacona grew grapes so that Cartier first named it Bacchus' Island before giving it its present-day name, the Island of Orleans. Birds were plentiful, and deer came to drink at the river in the evening. Fish and sea mammals, whales and seals were in great evidence.

On October 2, 1535, they finally arrived at Hochelaga, within sight of the mountain later named Mount Royal. The Indians flocked to meet them. "So soone as we were come neere Hochelaga, there came

*Painting of Francis I, King of France at the time of Jacques Cartier's voyages. Attributed to François Clouet.*
(Courtesy Musée du Louvre, Paris)

*Detail from a 1525 map of Normandy by Jean Jolivet showing typical Norman ships of the early sixteenth century.* (Courtesy Bibliothèque Nationale, Paris)

*Detail from the 1550 world map by Pierre Descalier showing a French galley on its way across the Atlantic under greatly reduced sail, possibly representing the ship of Jacques Cartier.* (Courtesy British Library)

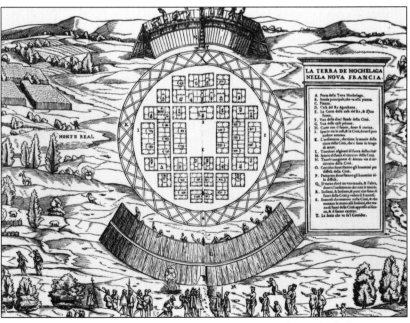

*Plan of Hochelaga, the fortified Indian town visited by Cartier before he climbed Mount Royal. The map was drawn after his first voyage in 1535, and was published in G.B. Ramusio's book* Navigationi et Viaggi *(Venice, 1556).* (Courtesy The Champlain Society)

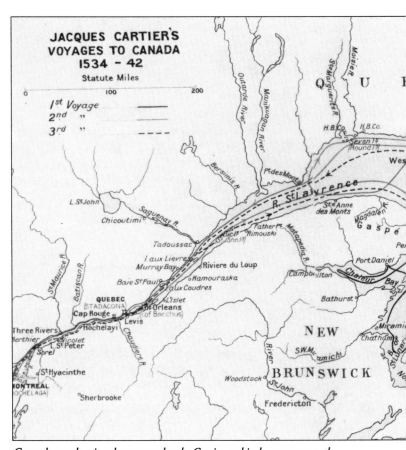

*General map showing the routes taken by Cartier on his three voyages to the St. Lawrence area.*

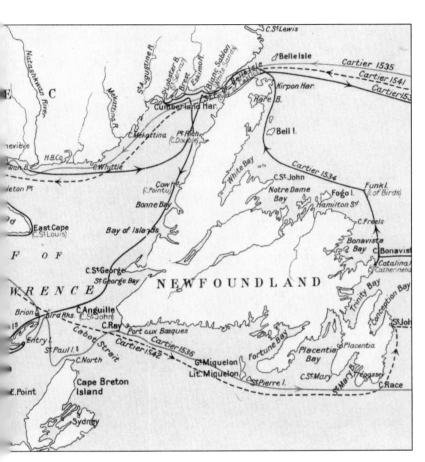

C.St Lewis
Belle Isle
Cartier 1535
Cartier 1541
Cartier 153
Natashkwan River
St Augustine R.
Lobster B.
Reservoir
Brest
Eskimo R.
Blanc Sablon
White Sands
Cumberland Har.
Kirpon Har.
Rare B.
Bell I.
Mekattina R.
C.Mekattina
Pt Riche
(C.Double)
White Bay
C.St John
Notre Dame Bay
Fogo I.
Funk I.
(I.of Birds)
Hamilton S.
enevieve
H.B.Co.
C.Whittle
wah B.
eton Pt
Cow Hd
(C.Point)
Bonne Bay
C.Freels
Cartier 1534
East Cape
(C.St Louis)
Bay of Islands
Bonavista Bay
C.Bonavist
Catalina
(C.Catherine)
F  OF
C.St George
St George Bay
NEWFOUNDLAND
Trinity Bay
RENCE
C.Anguille
(C.St John)
Conception Bay
St Joh
Brion I.
Bird Rks.
C.Ray
Port aux Basques
Cartier 1536
Fortune Bay
Placentia Bay
Placentia
s
Entry I.
St Paul I.
Cabot Strait
Cartier 1542
G. Miquelon
Lit. Miquelon
C.St Mary
St Pierre I.
Tregasse
C.Race
C.North
E.Point
Cape Breton Island
Sydney

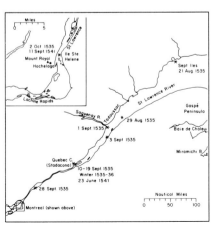

Detailed sketch map of the upper St.
Lawrence showing Cartier's movements
through the Quebec and Montreal areas.
(Drawing by Terry Dyer/based on a map
by W.F. Ganong)

Miles
0        5
2 Oct. 1535
11 Sept 1541
Mount Royal
Hochelaga
Ile Ste Helene
Sept Iles
21 Aug 1535
Lachine Rapids
St Lawrence River
Gaspé Peninsula
Saguenay R.
29 Aug. 1535
1 Sept 1535
Baie de Chaleu
3 Sept 1535
Miramichi B.
Quebec C.
(Stadacona)
10-19 Sept 1535
Winter 1535-36
23 June 1541
28 Sept 1535
Nautical Miles
0        50      100
Montreal (shown above)

to meete us above a thousand persons, men, women and children, who afterward did as friendly and merily entertaine and receive us as any father would doe his child, which he had not of long time seene, the men dauncing on one side, the women on another, and likewise the children on another: after that they brought us great store of fish & of their bread made of Millet, casting them into our boates so thicke, that you would have thought it to fall from heaven." On the following day they arose early to visit the village and to see "a certaine mountaine that is somewhat neer the citie."

Cartier was accompanied by five officers and twenty of his crew, the others being left to watch the boats. They walked inland several miles, finding the paths well beaten and passing between fields of corn which was similar to "the Millet of Brezil." In the middle of these fields they came upon "the citie of Hochelaga placed neere, and as it were joined to a great mountaine that is tilled round about, very fertill, on the top of which you may see very farre, we named it Mount Roiall."

The village of Hochelaga was enclosed by three high wooden stockades. It was a good strong defensive structure with only one entrance which could be barricaded with stakes and bars. Along the ramparts were platforms for defence with numerous ladders to provide access from the interior. The stockades enclosed about 50 bark-covered dwellings, each one close to 50 paces long and about 15 broad. Although the huts contained a variety of rooms, they all had a "great court, in the middle whereof they made their fire." On top were small storerooms for corn which was ground to make meal for bread. The houses also stored "certaine vessels as bigge as any But or Tun, wherein they preserve and keepe their fish, catching the same in sommer to be dried in the sunne, and live therewith in winter."

Cartier's party received a warm welcome. Mats were laid out for the guests to sit on, and the Indians brought out the sick to be cured, they hoped, by the touch of the white men. Cartier read from the Bible as he passed among the sick, and afterwards he distributed gifts to everyone present. The French spent only one day at Hochelaga but managed to find time to walk up Mount Royal. From the top, they had a spectacular view of the surrounding country spread out before them. Their Indian guides made signs towards the Ottawa River which

Cartier interpreted to mean that silver and gold could be found in that direction. A little farther to the south, the St. Lawrence stretched out, with the Lachine Rapids visible in the distance. Beyond these, they were informed, there were three other sets of rapids, after which the river could be navigated in boats. Here, perhaps, they might find the wealth they were looking for, but certainly there was no passage through to the East. However, it was now the beginning of October and too late in the season for further explanation. They returned to their boats and sailed downstream. Two days later they rejoined the *Emerillon,* and by October 11, Cartier was safely back with the other ships at Stadacona.

During the three-week absence of their commander, the men at Stadacona had set about making winter preparations. A stockade had been erected, and cannons had been brought from the ships for defence. For the few months before winter set in, they mixed freely with the Indians and learned about their way of life. The Indians remained friendly, but the suspicion grew among the French that the friendship was false and that if an opportunity presented itself, the Indians might try to take possession of the camp and its supplies. Accordingly, Cartier strengthened their small fort with a moat, closed all the gates through the stockade, except one, and mounted armed guards every night.

As the days passed, the temperature dropped. Winter gripped the land with a vigour which the French had never before experienced. From November until the middle of March, the ships were held fast in ice. In December, an "unknowen sicknes began to spread itselfe amongst us." Although unknown to Cartier at the time, his description shows clearly that his men were suffering from scurvy. "Some did lose all their strength and could not stand on their feete, then did their legges swel, their sinnowes shrinke as blacke as any cole ... then did it ascend up to their ankels, knees, thighes, shoulders, armes, and necke: their mouth became stincking, their gummes so rotten, that all the flesh did fall off, even to the rootes of the teeth, which did also almost all fall out."

By the middle of February, there were eight dead, fifty sick, and only ten men, including Cartier, still in good health. To their great good fortune, they were able to learn of a cure from some Indians they met on the ice. A potion was made by boiling the bark and needles of certain pine trees. The liquor was drunk and the dregs used as a poultice. At one time it was assumed that the potion contained vitamin C, but recently it has been found that pine needles contain only traces of vitamin C, and that there is absolutely none in the bark.[5] Instead, the trees contain a chemical which is an anti-oxidant, three times more effective than vitamin C. It certainly worked exceedingly well. A large tree was cut down, "as big as any oake in France." The bark and leaves were boiled, and "it wrought so well, that if all the physicians of Mountpelier and Lovaine had been there with all the drugs of Alexandria, they would not have done so much in one yere, as that tree did in sixe dayes."

While the French were ill, the Indian chief, Donnacona, had left the area, ostensibly to hunt for fresh meat. However, rather than being away for the two weeks or so, which he had indicated would be the length of the hunt, he was absent for nearly two months and returned with a large group of warriors. Relations with the Indians had gradually deteriorated throughout the winter. The French felt safe enough in their stockade, but the presence of so many warlike strangers made them suspect that they might have difficulty getting away without a fight. Rather than risk a direct confrontation, Cartier pretended that nothing was amiss and invited Donnacona and a few others to come aboard his ship for some final celebrations prior to sailing. As soon as the chief and all Cartier's men were safely on board, Cartier announced that he was leaving and was taking Donnacona with him. The Indians still on the shore were furious, but there was little they could do while the French sat tight in the safety of their ships with the Indian chief in custody.

Rather than leave with so much ill feeling, however, Cartier was able to win the chief's confidence with gifts and the assurance that he would bring him back the following year after having seen the delights of France. Having convinced Donnacona, Cartier could pacify the chief's followers, and the French were then able to make a safe and unhurried departure without storing up trouble for their return. On May 6 they set off downriver on their way back to France. They were delayed in the St. Lawrence River for some time by contrary winds, but these changed on May 21. They then sailed back along the Gaspé coast and out of the gulf along the south coast of Newfoundland. A quick crossing brought them safely back to St. Malo on July 16.

Cartier's achievements on this second voyage were considerable. He had sailed farther into the North American land mass than any other European. He had made extensive contacts with the native population, and from the top of Mount Royal, he had seen the route into the interior. But he had not found the wealth that his King had hoped for. In his view, Stadacona and Hochelaga were both primitive villages, and the Indians had nothing of any value.

The lands Cartier had discovered seemed ideal for developing colonies, but the King had no money for colonization, being involved in war with the Holy Roman Empire. Nevertheless, Cartier suggested, it still might be worthwhile to explore the Kingdom of Saguenay because of the silver and gold it was said to contain. The first hints of this potential wealth had been given to Cartier from the top of Mount Royal, and now, back in France, he and Donnacona proceeded to work on Francis's imagination. Donnacona described a land where people dressed like the French, where there were abundant jewels, gold and silver, and where it was only a "moneths sailing to go to a lande where cinnamon and cloves are gathered."

Both Francis and Cartier appear to have swallowed these stories wholesale, probably because they wanted desperately to believe them. Nevertheless, it was not until five years later that money could be spared to finance a third expedition.

This one was to be done in style. Ten ships were made available with 400 sailors and 300 soldiers. Provisions were arranged for a two-year voyage. Livestock was included, and masons, carpenters and ploughmen were engaged to settle the land of Canada and to explore "the countrey of Saguenay, whereof the people brought by Cartier made mention unto the King, that there were great riches."

The expedition proved close to being an unmitigated disaster. It was intended that Cartier would be accompanied by Jean François de la Roche, Sieur de Roberval, who would be the governor of the new colony, but Roberval was unable to get his ships ready in time.

Undoubtedly being frustrated with the constant delays, Cartier left St. Malo with five ships, but without Roberval's contingent, on May 23, 1541. It took them about three months to cross the Atlantic, and they had almost run out of water by the time they arrived, so much so that they had to water their cattle with cider!

After replenishing their water supply at a harbour near Belle Isle, they sailed through the Gulf to arrive at Stadacona on August 23. After the usual welcome they moved a few miles upriver, sent two ships home to provide news of their arrival, and erected forts for the winter.

As the forts were being constructed, the workmen discovered a "good store of stones, which we esteemed to be Diamants." A mine, "of the best yron in the world" was located, "and on the waters side we found certaine leaves of fine gold as thicke as a mans nayle." These were taken on board in large quantities. A later account of this collection indicated that it consisted of about ten barrels of "gold" ore, several barrels of silver and "close on a bushel of precious stones, rubies and diamonds." Testing eventually showed them all to be worthless, but not until they arrived back in France.

At the beginning of September, Cartier took two of the ship's boats up the St. Lawrence, as far as Hochelaga, to investigate the rapids he had found on his previous visits. How much he learned is unknown, but on his way back, he heard rumours that the Indians were planning to raid the settlement. When his party arrived back at the fort, their suspicions were confirmed by the news that the Indians had stopped coming to trade, "wherefore our captaine ... [knowing] that there were a wonderfull number of the Countrey people assembled together, caused all things in our fortress to be set in good order."

No further information about this voyage exists. Despite the problems of ice and snow, the expedition did survive the winter, but the colonists had evidently had enough, and sailed back to France in the following spring, a year earlier than planned.

Meanwhile, Roberval, after extensive delays, had managed to get under way in April 1542. Purely by chance, the two parts of the original expedition met up again in June, in St. John's harbour. Roberval was then getting ready to journey up the St. Lawrence, whereas Cartier was on his way home. Roberval argued that they should combine forces and return upriver for another year, but Cartier refused and, according to Roberval's account, "stole privily away the next night from us," so that his crew would get "all the glory of the discoverie of those partes themselves."

The account was somewhat biased, of course, and it is just as likely that Cartier was simply fed up, both with the dangers posed by the Indians and with the frustration and difficulty of dealing with Roberval, who had taken over a year to get organized. At any rate, Cartier now sailed for home, eager to have his mineral finds tested and laid before the King. Of course, these proved to be worthless. Indeed, his belief that he had discovered diamonds became so ridiculed that the catch phrase "Voilà un Diamant de Canada" passed into the culture of the day, and became a well known saying to describe fraudulent and misleading claims.

After Cartier's departure, Roberval pressed on to make another attempt to colonize the area around the head of the St. Lawrence. Nothing came of it. Following another cold and miserable winter, he investigated the Saguenay River for some ten miles and considered pushing on up the St. Lawrence past the Lachine Rapids to winter again in the interior. His narrative about this expedition provides no further information, but he obviously turned back, for he is known to have been back in France in the autumn of 1543.

The debacle of the third voyage put an end to French exploration in North America for almost sixty years. Francis lost interest in this land of ice and snow, which had provided no return on his considerable investment, and besides, until the end of the century, the French were caught up in domestic turmoil with little time or money for New World discovery. No accounts are available to describe the remaining fifteen years of Cartier's life. As far as is known, he received no further commissions and died, still held in great public esteem, in 1557. Only later would the importance of his voyages be recognized, and only long after his death would he be hailed as the discoverer of Canada.

# CHAPTER FIVE

# THE ELIZABETHAN THRUST

*F*or almost forty years after Hoare's 1536 voyage to Cape Breton and southern Newfoundland, there was little English interest in New World exploration. Merchants were getting little or no financial return from their investments, and more pressing problems occupied the court's attention, especially the deteriorating relations between King Henry VIII and the Pope. In these years Spain replaced France as England's major enemy. Anglo-Spanish trade decreased, and suspicion grew between the two nations as privateering increased. At the same time, England's economy began to suffer, largely because of difficulties in the wool trade. There was great concern over England's dependence on Spain for oils and dyes, and the increase in Spain's own wool production presented a direct threat to the English economy. At the same time, many people perceived Spanish strength as deriving directly from her American colonies, and the idea of planting colonies in parts of America not yet under Spanish control began to grow.

Many influential men in Court believed that overseas colonies were the answer to all of England's problems. Seeing that the Spanish had confined themselves to the south, England believed "that the countries lying to the North of Florida, God hath reserved ... to be reduced to Christian civility by the English nation."[1]

Colonies would bring employment and ensure that "lustie youthes," who were then "turned to no profitable vse," would find jobs and security rather than turn to disorder and rebellion. Indeed, the possibility of widespread rioting was increasing. Recurring inflation led to rising food prices, low wages and a growing number of discontented landless peasants, all of whom could find a place in the colonies.

The idealized picture of England populated by busy merchants and contented workers "full of good belly cheer" was quite false. During most of Henry VIII's reign,[2] labourers were paid only about five pence a day at a time when a wool cap or a pair of the poorest quality shoes cost one shilling (twelve pence). Employment was mostly casual, and with luck a man might find work for only half the available working days. Few people owned their own homes, and 5 percent of the population owned about 80 percent of the wealth. Landowners were about 30 times better off than the average workingman and the aristocracy was between 400 and 2,000 times better off. Conditions were no better in rural areas. The poor faced starvation whenever the harvest failed—a common occurrence. Wheat prices rose rapidly after a bad harvest—by as much as two and a half times between 1525 and 1527 — and most people in rural areas had little or no income.

People either starved or turned to stealing and petty thievery, which often had the same result, as the punishment for theft was hanging. Indeed, with an estimated total of 72,000 people executed during Henry VIII's reign, hanging constituted one of the most common causes of death! Things improved with prolonged peacetime after King Henry's death, but there was still concern over the potential problems which might be caused by the indigent poor.

The establishment of colonies, however, would do more than provide work for idle malcontents. Colonies would open up new markets closely tied to England and would re-energize the wool trade. They would stimulate shipping at a time when most English people counted the strength of their country in terms of the number of merchant ships.

Although Henry VIII had by then created the Royal Navy, it was not until much later that a distinction was made between merchant and naval ships. During the early Tudor era, all the fleets which were organized for war contained a majority of privately owned ships, and even as late as the Spanish Armada in 1588, the public was still of this opinion, although seamen themselves knew that most of the fighting was done by Queen Elizabeth's ships.

The stimulation and encouragement of shipbuilding was, therefore, tied directly to the ability of the nation to withstand invasion and to repel foreign fleets. Another factor was the increasing importance of the North Atlantic fishery, not only for food but also for employment. During Queen Elizabeth's reign, more than 10,000 men were employed in the fishery, and at one point, more than half the national revenue was obtained directly from fish.

While some saw the coastline of North America as a place for colonization, others saw it as a possible route to Cathay with all the attending trade benefits. The search for a northern passage was necessitated by Portuguese control of the southern routes. Initially, it was of far greater importance than the possibility of colonization of the New World, and only later, when the search came to nothing, did England turn to conquest and occupation of North America.

The first push to discover a northern passage was towards the east, going north around Russia. Among other reasons for this choice, men argued that no wool could be sold to the native inhabitants of America, while there might well be civilized people of Chinese origin along the northeastern route.

A joint stock company of merchant adventurers sent out an expedition of three ships in 1553. It failed to reach China and got only as far as Russia. Other ships that followed confirmed that the obstacles on this route were insurmountable, and their interest in China largely evaporated. The company changed its name to reflect its new focus. It became known as the Muscovy Company and set to work to develop trade links with the court of Ivan the Terrible in Moscow.

However, interest in a western route to China was still being kindled in some influential circles. Many of the original enthusiasts for the northern passage had died, but one of the principals who remained was Dr. John Dee, a brilliant Welsh intellectual who had risen to great heights in Court circles. He was acknowledged as England's greatest authority on the mathematics of navigation, but was also an accomplished geographer, putting out maps, handbooks and essays on navigation, all of which were eagerly sought after. In addition, he was a known astrologer and necromancer, and gossip suggested he practised black magic in return for the assistance of demons.

He had staunchly supported the search for a northeast passage, but when it became obvious that this had failed, he just as enthusiastically supported setting up a new search in the Northwest. In this venture he was joined by Sir Humphrey Gilbert, a West Countryman, half-brother of the young Walter Raleigh. Together they built a convincing case which culminated in Gilbert's publication, in 1576, of *Discourse of a Discovery for a New Passage to Cathaia,* in which he presented all the available evidence for the existence of a northwest passage. Although many of his arguments were simplistic and unfounded, the *Discourse* shows that his research was thorough and that he had a good knowledge of the information and maps then available. Gilbert's discourse emphasized the economic advantages of a northwest passage and suggested the possibility of colonization.

The *Discourse* was written in 1566, ten years before it was published, and it is thought that Gilbert brought it out in 1576 primarily to support Michael Locke and Martin Frobisher, who were encouraging the Muscovy Company to renew the search for a passage to China. Frobisher took the lead and, with Elizabeth's support, approached the company in 1574 for a licence to make the attempt. There was some initial resistance, but when he returned again the following year with stronger support from the Queen, a licence was reluctantly granted. Lack of patrons and funds delayed his departure, but eventually, in June 1576, Frobisher set out with two small twenty-five-ton ships, the *Gabriel* and the *Michael,* and one small ten-ton pinnace. A month later, when they reached Greenland, the pinnace sank in a storm. Shortly afterwards the *Michael* gave up and ran for home. Frobisher, in the *Gabriel,* continued up the coast of Labrador and entered waters now known as Frobisher Bay, in Baffin Island. At the time, not realizing that this large expanse of water was landlocked, he named it Frobisher Straits thinking he had discovered the passage to the East.

Frobisher landed and made contact with the Inuit, who appeared to be friendly. There appeared to be so little danger that five of the crew later took the only ship's boat ashore. They were never heard of again, and with only thirteen men left to man his ship and no boat, Frobisher decided to return to England. Before leaving, however, he kidnapped a native in retaliation for the loss of his five crewmen. The unfortunate man was enticed to sail his kayak out to the *Gabriel* by hanging a bell over the side. When he arrived to take it, Frobisher bent over the side and, in a prodigious feat of strength, "caught the man fast, and plucked him with maine force, boate and al, into his bark out of the sea."[3]

In England, Frobisher's accounts of the voyage created such wild excitement that a new company, the Company of Cathay, was immediately formed to exploit his discovery. Locke was appointed governor for the next six years and contributed £300 to the venture. Even the thrifty Queen Elizabeth was so impressed with the news that she invested £1,000 in the company. No doubt a large part of this enthusiasm stemmed from the fact that Frobisher had brought back ore which was believed to contain gold.

With this support, he made a second voyage and reached Frobisher Bay in the middle of July 1577. He stayed only about five weeks—long enough to load 200 tons of ore, which he brought back for assay. Preliminary results varied but were sufficiently encouraging for him to make another voyage in May 1578, this time with fifteen ships.

By now the idea of discovery had taken second place to mining, and over a period of about two months they loaded 1,300 tons of ore into the ships. Leaving Baffin Island at the beginning of August, they arrived back only to face disaster. The three voyages had cost approximately £20,000, all raised by private subscription, and a considerable portion had remained upaid. Worse than this was the news that assays had proved the ore was worthless. Locke was put in a debtor's prison. The stockholders of the company went bankrupt, and Frobisher himself appears to have turned pirate for a time. Later he seems to have redeemed himself in the service of the Crown and fought against the Spaniards at the Armada and later at Brent, in 1594, where he died of wounds.

Gilbert was not closely involved in the dealings of the Company of Cathay, and by 1577 he seems to have given up the idea of looking for a northwest passage. Indeed, there is good reason to suggest that his ideas had changed soon after he wrote his *Discourse* and well before its publication. In 1567, he went to Ireland in service of the Crown, where he stayed for three years. English plans to conquer Ulster resulted in the final large-scale suppression in 1566, in which Gilbert earned a reputation for his ruthlessness. He said he believed "that no conquered nation will ever yield willingly their obedience for love but rather for fear." Following this dictum he was totally heartless in his dealings with the Irish. If a castle did not submit to him at his first demand, he made a point of killing everything in it—men, women, children and animals—when he finally forced entry. Irish lords who came to surrender were made to walk to his tent through a row of severed heads stuck on pikes.[4]

During this time he seems to have hit on the idea of placing settlers there to advance England's interests, and the potential advantages of this idea were equally applicable to English colonies in America. Indeed, he was the first Englishman to indicate the possibility in print and, in addition to promoting the northwest passage, his *Discourse* of 1576 suggested that "we might inhabit some part of those countries" and "settle there such needie people of our country."[5]

After Gilbert served as a member of Parliament and had seen further military service, he was back in England in time to throw his support behind the renewed activity for exploration in the Northwest. In November 1577, he prepared a series of proposals to the Queen, including a discourse on "how her Majesty might annoy the king of Spain by fitting out a fleet of warships under pretense of a voyage of discovery and so fall upon the enemy shipping destroying his trade in Newfoundland and the West Indies, and possess both regions."[6]

A second expedition would join the first and proceed to ravage the West Indies, capture Spanish galleons and then occupy Cuba and Santo Domingo in order to establish an English colony. Elizabeth's response to these suggestions was carefully worded. Gilbert was given the patents he requested and was encouraged to "discover searche find out and viewe such remote heathen and barbarous landes countries and territories not actually possessed by any Christian Prince or people as to him … shall seeme good. And the same to have, holde occupie and enjoye to him his heires and assignes forever."[7]

Having provided what was effectively the first English colonial charter, Elizabeth was careful to distance herself from the original objective, and specifically ordered Gilbert not to attack any foreign ships or colonies. Whether there were other, secret orders has never become clear. Ships were prepared, but the objective of the voyage was kept secret, although it does seem that Gilbert did not intend to sail to Newfoundland at that time. It has been suggested that he was interested, instead, in establishing a colony between Cape Hatteras and the mouth of the Hudson River. There are also some indications that he planned a voyage to more southerly latitudes, but nothing is certain.

Gilbert had intended to leave during the summer of 1578, but his ships did not assemble until late August. There were other delays— three of his captains deserted and took their ships off to become pirates—so it was not until November that he sailed from Dartmouth with the seven remaining vessels. What happened next is not very clear, but a combination of bad weather (due to the approaching winter), low supplies and poorly equipped ships aborted the expedition. Gilbert returned to England hoping to proceed again in the following summer. However, the Privy Council issued orders preventing a renewal of the expedition, probably because of the piracy in the preceding year, and the government found alternative uses for some of the remaining ships.

Running short of funds, Gilbert devised various new projects to improve his financial situation, one of which was to set up a colony for English Catholics, and another, an attempt to raise money from the town of Southampton by promising that it would be the trading centre for the new colonies. The Queen, however, would not allow the Catholics to leave England because the Catholic nobility owed money to the Crown. Gilbert did raise money from Southampton and was almost ready to proceed when, in February 1583, Elizabeth tried to persuade him to cancel his plans on the basis that his previous seagoing experience did not bode well for the future. Gilbert managed to overcome her objections, however, and in March, Walter Raleigh wrote on her behalf saying, "she wished great good hap and safety to your ships as if herself were there in person."[8]

He finally got under way in June 1583, and sailed with a fleet of five ships, the largest being the *Raleigh* (200 tons) and the smallest the *Squirrill*(10 tons). Sir Humphrey Gilbert sailed in the flagship *Delight* (120 tons). The *Raleigh* carried the vice-admiral's flag, and the *Golden Hinde* (40 tons) took the place of rear admiral. One other ship, the *Swallow*, was a tiny barque the same size as the *Squirrill*.

Gilbert's voyage was significant for two reasons: first, it resulted in England acquiring its first overseas possession—Newfoundland—and second, but no less important, it was a forerunner of the vast colonies and dominations which were to follow. This is intimated in the information provided by one of Gilbert's captains, Sir Edward Haies, who later wrote an extensive report of the voyage noting its intention "to discover and to plant Christian inhabitants in place convenient, upon those large and ample countreys extended North-ward from the cape of Florida, lying under very temperate Climes, esteemed fertile and rich in Minerals, yet not in the actuall possession of any Christian prince."[9]

Gilbert's first problem was to determine a course across the Atlantic. Many factors suggested a southerly route towards Florida, allowing them to take advantage of the currents running north along the coastline and assisting in their primary purpose of discovery. At the same time, they would have the benefit of wintering in the south. However, despite these advantages, there was one serious disadvantage. Gilbert had again experienced problems in outfitting the ships and he was short on supplies. As a result, his captains worried about the dangers of a long southerly voyage that necessitated providing food through the winter.

The alternative route was to sail north directly towards Newfound-land. This was a much shorter crossing, and "at that time of the year, and until the five of August, a multitude of ships" were fishing in the vicinity so that the fleet could be resupplied on its arrival. This course was not chosen lightly. Gilbert intended to remain in Newfoundland for the shortest possible time before proceeding to the south, for he was well aware that the "sudden approach of Winter, bringing with it continuall fogge, and thicke mists, tempest and rage of weather; also contrariety of currents descending from the Cape of Florida unto

*"Humfridus Gilbertus Miles Auratus Etc," a portrait of Sir Humphrey Gilbert from* Herwologia Anglica, *by Henry Holland (London, 1620). Sir Humphrey's motto* Quid Non *(why not), is clearly shown.*
(Courtesy British Library)

*A portrait of Martin Frobisher by an unknown artist, 1577. A Yorkshireman, Frobisher became famous for his three Arctic voyages, 1576-1578. He later commanded a ship against the Armada and died at the hands of the Spanish in 1594.*
(Courtesy Bodleian Library, Oxford)

*Portrait of Dr. John Dee, Elizabethan geographer and necromancer, 1792. Dee was one of the chief proponents of English discovery and colonization and was the first person to use the term "British Empire."* (Courtesy Trustees of the British Museum)

*The frontispiece of John Dee's* General and Rare Memorials pertayning to the Perfect Arte of Navigation, *showing Queen Elizabeth at the helm of the Christian ship of Europe.* (Courtesy British Library)

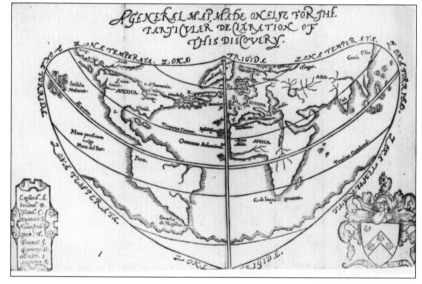

A GENERAL MAP, MADE ONELYE FOR THE PARTICULER DECLARATION OF THIS DISCOVERY

# SALT

## AND

# FISHERY,

*A Discourse thereof*

Insisting on the following HEADS.

1. The several ways of making Salt in *England*, and Foreign Parts.
2. The *Character* and *Qualities* good and bad, of these several sorts of *Salt*, English refin'd asserted to be much better than any Foreign.
3. The *Catching* and *Curing*, or *Salting* of the most Eminent or Staple sorts of *Fish*, for long or short keeping.
4. The Salting of *Flesh*.
5. The Cookery of *Fish* and *Flesh*.
6. Extraordinary Experiments in preserving *Butter*, *Flesh*, *Fish*, *Fowl*, *Fruit*, and *Roots*, fresh and sweet for long keeping.
7. The Case and Sufferings of the *Saltworkers*.
8. Proposals for their *Relief*, and for the advancement of the *Fishery*, the *Woollen*, *Tin*, and divers other *Manufactures*.

By *JOHN COLLINS*, Accomptant to the ROYAL FISHERY Company.

*E Reg. Soc. Philomath.*

*LONDON*, Printed by *A. Godbid* and *J. Playford*, 1682

*By 1682, when this "Discourse" was published, Newfoundland had become a prime source of cod for English fishermen. Large numbers of West Countrymen were employed in the fishery, which had become a mainstay of the English economy. As a result, merchants were most receptive to "Discourses" which explained the operations.* (Courtesy Memorial University)

Facing page, top: *Woodcut, 1580, showing Inuit hunting seabirds from their summer encampment. Probably based on a drawing by John White, who accompanied Martin Frobisher on his second voyage to the Arctic. From "De Martini Frobisseri Angli navigatione in Regiones occidentis et Septentrionis Narratio historica," by Dionyse Settle.* (Courtesy British Library)

Facing page, bottom: *Sir Humphrey Gilbert's map of the world from* A Discourse of a Discovery for a New Passage to Cathaia *(London, 1576). This "general map made onelye for the particular declaration of this discovery" is drawn on a cordiform projection and shows a northern passage to Quinzay (Quingit), China (Mangi), and Japan (Giapon).* (Courtesy British Library)

Cape Briton and Cape Rase, would fall out to be great and irresistable impediments unto our further proceeding for that year, and compell us to Winter in those North and colde regions."

The dangers of the voyage were not limited to the winter, and there was the ever-present worry that they might be attacked. Accordingly, when the course and the orders had been determined, these were given to the captain of each ship in two packages, one sealed in wax and the other left open. Both packets included the necessary watchwords. The open packet contained those which would be used until the fleet had cleared the Irish coast, after which the watchwords in the closed packet would be used. These simple codes would allow the various ships to recognize each other if the fleet became separated and met up again in fog or at night. At the same time, the division of the packets protected them "lest any of the company stealing from the fleet might bewray the same: which knowen to any enemy, he might boord us by night without mistrust, having our own watch-word."

Haies provides details of eleven orders agreed upon by the captains of the fleet. These consisted of methods of signalling at night, showing different lights and different numbers of lights to indicate, for example, the raising or lowering of sails. Gunfire was to be used if any ship ran into danger, and attention was paid to the probability that they would experience poor weather. Alternative rendezvous were arranged to cope with contrary winds, and special marks were given for identification in case a ship landed but had to leave the rendezvous before the rest of the fleet could arrive. Fog was an ever-present danger that was dealt with in some detail. "If it shall happen a great fogge to fall then presently every shippe to beare up with the Admirall, if there be winde: but if it be calm then every ship to hull, and so to lie at hull till it be cleare. And if the fogge do continue long, then the Admirall to shoot off two pieces every evening, and every ship to answere it with one shot: and every man bearing to the ship, that is to leeward so neere as he may."

The fleet set out from Causand Bay near Plymouth in good weather on Tuesday, June 11. There were about 260 men, including shipwrights, masons, carpenters, and smiths, together with "minerall men and refiners." On a long dangerous voyage of discovery it was necessary to keep up the sailors' spirits, and where trade or settlement was intended, some method of making friends with the natives was required. Thus "for solace of our people and allurement of the Savages, we were provided of Musike in good variety: not omitting the least toyes, as Morris dancers, Hobby horsse, and Maylike conceits to delight the Savage people, whom we intended to winne by all faire means possible. And to that end we were indifferently furnished of all petty haberdasherie wares to barter with those people."

Almost immediately the expedition met with misfortune. On Thursday, within two days of the order to sail, the captain and many of the men on board the *Raleigh* became sick with a contagious disease. They were so ill that the *Raleigh* was forced to return to Plymouth, leaving Sir Edward's ship, the *Golden Hinde*, to take its place as vice-admiral.

Throughout June the weather steadily worsened—"we never had faire day without fogge or raine, and windes bad, much to the West Northwest." Their original plan had been first to hold south to a latitude of between 43°N and 44°N and then to move into more northerly latitudes, between 46° N and 47° N. However, on leaving the coast of Ireland, the wind drove them south—to 41°N, before it changed and they were forced to run much farther north than they intended—as much as 51°N.

Together with contrary winds, they experienced "much fogge and mists in maner palpable, in which we could not keepe so well together, but were disseevered, losing the company of the *Swallow* and the *Squirrill* upon the 20 day of July." The three larger ships sailed on together, and being so far north, they were soon accompanied by "mountaines of ice driven upon the sea." These icebergs are common in the sea lanes off Newfoundland in July and were noted as being "carried southward to the weather of us." From their direction, Sir Edward conjectured that "some current doth set that way from the north"—the Labrador Current.

Seven weeks after leaving the coast of England, they sighted some land and estimated that they were about 51°N. If their reckoning was correct, they were then lying off the northern tip of the island of Newfoundland, or perhaps off the southern part of Labrador. The haze and fog lying off the coast, however, was so thick that they could neither measure the latitude nor see the shore with any clarity. Nothing was seen "but hideous rockes and mountaines, bare of trees and voide of any green herbe."

Following the coast south, they again met with the *Swallow* in Conception Bay, Newfoundland. To their surprise they found that she was apparently still well stocked after the long voyage, and that the crew had managed to acquire a completely new set of clothing. They soon learned that this had been obtained from a chance encounter with a boat returning from the fishing grounds. On its arrival at the coast, the *Swallow* had almost run out of food and the crew was short of clothing and other tackle. Their captain permitted the men to go aboard the fishing boat "only to borrow what might be spared" but once on board, the men had rifled "tackle, sailes, cables, victuals, and the men of their apparell: not sparing by torture [winding cords about their heads] to draw out what else they thought good." Sir Edward castigated the crew for their actions but mentions, almost in passing, that the whole business was hardly surprising because of the nature of the crew. Indeed, the *Swallow* and most of its crew had initially been commandeered off the coast of England when they were surprised in an act of piracy raiding two French ships!

Still sailing south, the expedition met up with the *Squirrill* off St. John's harbour, which they entered on Saturday, August 3. The harbour has a very narrow entrance and provides a large, fully enclosed, safe anchorage. Inside, they found thirty-six ships from various nations and, with a number of English vessels there for the fishing, they had no difficulty replenishing their stocks. Indeed, soon after arriving, they were presented with "wines, marmalads, most fine ruske or bisket, sweet oyles, sundry delicasies … fresh salmons, trouts, lobsters and other fresh fish."

The next day, Gilbert summoned the merchants and masters of all ships in the harbour (both English and foreign) and read them his commission, "by vertue whereof he tooke possession in the same harbour of St. John's and 200 leagues every way," in the name of Elizabeth, "and signified unto al men that from that time forward, they should take the same land as a territorrie appertaining to the

Queene of England." Laws were proclaimed for the governance of the territory and the arms of England were set up, "ingraven in lead and infixed upon a pillar of wood."

The small fleet remained in St. John's for just over two weeks, during which time Sir Humphrey gathered as much information concerning the island as possible. Even in this short time, he had to face the typical problems which arose at any landfall after a long voyage. Many of his men were plotting mischief. Some deserted and hid in the woods intending to return home on a fishing ship. There was considerable raiding and theft, and, in perhaps the most extreme case, a gang of Sir Humphrey's men overpowered a ship laden with fish, set the original crew on shore and sailed off. Many of the seamen came down with illness. Some died, and the general result of the desertions and afflictions was such that they had too few men left to man the four ships. Therefore, before departing from St. John's, Sir Humphrey decided to leave one ship, the *Swallow*, to take the sick back to England while he and the other two explored south along the coast. Having made this decision, the depleted fleet left St. John's on Tuesday, August 20. By the following night they were at Cape Race, about sixty-five miles to the south. There they were becalmed and spent some time fishing. The banks of Newfoundland were well known by English fishermen, and laying out "hookes and lines to take Codde [they] drew in lesse than two houres, fish so large and in such abundance, that many dayes after we fed upon no other provision."

Gilbert's intention was to head for Sable Island, to the south of Cape Breton, where cattle and pigs were reputed to be thriving after being set ashore thirty years previously. Initially, he stayed close to the Newfoundland shore exploring the inlets and bays and sending "men on land to take view of the soyle along the coast." Good reports were received, so much so that some of the crew "had a wil to be planted there." As they continued on across the gulf towards Cape Breton, the weather remained "indifferent good" for several days, but on Thursday, August 29, the wind rose and a gale started up with rain and thick fog. By the following morning they found themselves in shallow water, and the sea was so white and broken that the master of Sir Edward's ship, the *Golden Hinde*, thought he could see white cliffs.

Their largest ship, the *Delight*, was closest to the breakers and ran aground before it could get any sea room. The other two ships, the *Golden Hinde*, carrying Sir Edward Haies, and the *Squirrill*, with Sir Humphrey Gilbert, bore south into the wind and beat up and down the coast for the rest of that day "as near unto the wracke as was possible for us, looking out, if good hap we might espie any of them." It proved impossible to attempt a rescue, however, and they later learned that the captain and almost a hundred men had perished. Only a few escaped in a small boat, about the size of a Thames barge, and were able to make their way to safety over the next six days.

The two ships which escaped from the gale, particularly the smaller *Squirrill*, were now in dire straits. The weather continued to be "thicke and blustery," the temperature was dropping, and there was still shallow water on their lee side with inevitable danger if the wind freshened again. Worst of all, their provisions were running short, and with the largest ship gone, there was no hope of supply. The men in the *Squirrill* were almost destitute, and Sir Humphrey was persuaded to return to England "before they all perished." In the poor weather, communications were difficult and the men had to make their distress known by "pointing to their mouthes and to their clothes, thinne and ragged."

Having consulted with the remaining two captains, Sir Humphrey ordered the two ships turned about on the afternoon of Saturday, August 31. With high winds and in a rough sea, they sailed up to Cape Race within a couple of days, a journey which had taken them four times as long on their way south. Sir Humphrey had been sailing in the *Squirrill*, it being the smallest ship and most convenient for exploring harbours and creeks, but he boarded the *Golden Hinde* on Monday to have a small foot injury dressed by the surgeon. Both the captain of the *Golden Hinde* and Captain Haies were concerned for his safety if he returned to the *Squirrill*, which Haies felt was carrying too much tackle and too many guns. The smallest of the original five ships, it was really too small and overloaded for an ocean voyage so late in the season. But Gilbert decided to return, remarking that he would not "foresake my little company going homeward, with whom I have passed so many stormes and perils." He did, however, agree that both ships would carry lights throughout the hours of darkness so that they could at least keep together.

Sailing north until they reached a latitude around 50°N, about that of the English Channel, they met extremely bad weather with high, steep waves. This continued for over a week, until Monday, September 9, when the *Squirrill* nearly foundered north of the Azores. As it recovered from the squall, the *Golden Hinde* sailed over to see if the crew needed assistance. Sir Humphrey was seen sitting aft with a book in his hand, and as they came within earshot, he waved to reassure them and was heard to cry, "We are as neere to heaven by sea as by land." It was the last they saw of him. On the same evening, about midnight, the lights of the *Squirrill* suddenly disappeared and all sight of her was lost. Despite a good search they found no trace of wreckage or survivors and the *Golden Hinde* reluctantly moved on. Thirteen days later they sailed up the English Channel in thick fog and landed at Falmouth.

Gilbert's voyage led directly to further English interest in colonization, and his ideas were taken up and expanded by men of action such as his half-brother, Walter Raleigh. But others, such as John Dee and Richard Hakluyt, to whom the pen was at least as mighty as the sword, were equally important. Dee wrote a considerable amount on the benefits of settlement, but one of the most influential publications of the period was the book by Richard Hakluyt, a Hertfordshire scholar and cleric, entitled *The Principall Navigations and Discoveries of the English Nation*—"made by sea or ouerland to the most remote and farthest distant Quarters of the earth at any time within the compasse of these 1500 years." Published in 1589 and running to over 700,000 words, it was intended to advertise the English voyages and to imbue Englishmen with an understanding and enthusiasm for colonization. Over the next ten years, so many voyages took place that the work became outdated. Undaunted, Hakluyt set to work again and added another million words for the second edition, which appeared at the end of the century.

Gilbert, Raleigh, Richard Hakluyt and John Dee, who was the first to coin the phrase "British Empire," probably did more than any other group to push England towards colonizaton.[10] Dee and Hakluyt never ventured far from England, but their compelling advocacy of an expansionist policy, coupled with the initial practical steps taken by Gilbert and Raleigh, set England on a path which would lead straight to the Empire on which the sun never set. Richard Hakluyt died in 1616. By then Queen Elizabeth had also died, but the future seemed clear, and her people took pride because it seemed to them that their forebears, "in searching the most opposite corners of the world and, to speak, plainly, in compassing the vast globe of the earth more than once, have excelled all nations and peoples of the earth."[11]

CHAPTER SIX

# $T$HE BASQUE WHALERS

$W$hen Sir Humphrey Gilbert sailed into St. John's harbour in 1583, his arrival and annexation of the area in the name of Queen Elizabeth must have been greeted with some cynicism, and not merely because he ran aground in the narrow harbour entrance! As indicated in the previous chapter, there were more than thirty fishing vessels in the harbour when he finally managed to berth, and most of these were French or Portuguese. The English were relative latecomers to the area, which was already well known to fishermen from the west coast of Europe. Shortly after the initial discovery by John Cabot in 1500, Gaspar Corte Réal, a Portuguese mariner, sailed to the coast of Newfoundland. His first voyage was followed up by an expedition in 1501 with three ships, and then again in 1502 with two ships under the command of his brother Miguel. Both Réal brothers were lost somewhere on the high seas, but fishermen followed in their wake, and it is likely that their voyages gave impetus to the growth of the Portuguese fishery.

By 1506 the Portuguese were familiar with the excellent fishing in the area which they called "Terra Nova," later known to the Spaniards as "Tierra Neuva" and to the French as "Terre-Neufsve." In Cartier's first voyage, of 1534, he explored the east, west and north coasts of Newfoundland. A year later he returned on his way to his first landing in New France, and at that time he completed a circumnavigation of the island.

For many years, however, the geography was quite unclear. Early maps show the area as an extension of Asia in the form of a large horn protruding into the ocean. This idea eventually gave way to a group

93

of islands separated by a number of channels which, at about the end of the century, the mapmakers resolved into one island lying a few miles east of the continental land mass.

In the early part of the sixteenth century, there was plenty of space available in the area for fishermen from all four countries (Portugal, Spain, France and England), and many small harbours were shared amicably. Gradually, however, different nations began to select areas of the coastline for their own, sometimes exclusive activities. In the 1530s and 1540s, most of the English used the coastline from a point south of Cape Spear, the most easterly land in North America, to the area around St. John's harbour. French fishermen were prominent north of St. John's and to the west and south of the Avalon Peninsula. There they shared the harbours with Basques, and in time, the town of Placentia, named after the medieval Basque town of Placencia (now Plencia), developed as a centre for fish drying. The almost landlocked harbour of St. John's became a rendezvous for ships of the different nations. There they could shelter in safety and could obtain food and other stores when they came off the Grand Banks laden with fish.

With the necessity for maintaining some law and order, a system of fishing admirals developed whereby the captain of the first ship to dock at the beginning of the fishing season became the "governor" of the surrounding area. He had the right to assign landing and working areas to ships arriving later and could exert considerable control over all fishing and associated activities in and around the harbour. By about 1580, English activity in the vicinity of St. John's had developed to the point that it was understood that the admiral would be from an English ship. This dominance may well have paved the way for Sir Humphrey's unopposed annexation. However, the influence of the English was somewhat limited at that time and had been very late in coming. For many years before the English became established on the Grand Banks, Portuguese ships were plentiful and French and Basque fishermen were much in evidence.

Although suggestions have been made that Basque fishermen were on the coast before John Cabot (similar claims have been made for Bristol merchants), documentary evidence indicates that the first

Basque expeditions were made in search of cod during the 1520s. In early years they concentrated entirely on cod fishing, but soon they learned that abundant numbers of whales passed through these waters, and by the middle of the century, they were looking for profits from both. Whaling stations were established in harbours around the west coast of Newfoundland, up through the Strait of Belle Isle, along the southern shore of Labrador and in other parts of the Gulf. Indeed, many of the place names still used on the western coast of Newfoundland are of Basque origin.

By the time of Gilbert's arrival off the coast in 1583, at least nine whaling stations were in operation about four hundred miles north of St. John's. One of these, Red Bay in Labrador, is estimated to have had a summer population of between six and nine hundred men employed in what had become a thriving industry.

Throughout the sixteenth century, the Basques were known as hardy fishermen and successful whalers. Living in an area at the southeast corner of the Bay of Biscay, close to the French and Spanish borders, the Basques are distinct from both the Spanish and the French. They refer to themselves as Euskaldunak, which literally translates as "the speakers of Euskera," a language with no known relationship to any other language. Cultural differences are complemented by physical differences, particularly remarked by their variations in blood groupings from other, surrounding peoples. Present-day Basques, for example, have a significantly lower percentage of blood group B and a significantly higher percentage of blood group O than any other European population. The incidence of the Rhesus negative factor is the highest of any population in the world, reaching as high as 27.5 percent in the area around Bilbao.

Although it is impossible to date the beginning of Basque whaling with any certainty, the area the Basques inhabited was used by sailors in Roman times when some of the natural harbours were frequented by Mediterranean shipping. Whales seem to have been plentiful along the coast, and their presence in the Bay of Biscay was described as early as the fourth century, when Ausonius of Bordeaux mentioned them in his chronicles. The presence of dead whales beached on the shore was noted (he suggested that they had been blown ashore), and it is likely that local inhabitants would learn the value of the oil, meat and bones from these accidental gifts of the sea.

In the Roman era, southwestern Europe depended almost entirely for its oil supply on the olive trees growing in countries around the Mediterranean. With the decline of the Roman Empire, however, the supply of olive oil dried up, and whale oil proved to be the best substitute. Whale oil came to be in great demand in the Frankish kingdom, where there was an extensive need, not only for lamps, but also for the production of soap and for the preparation of woollen and leather clothing. As early as the seventh century, there are references to Basques selling whale oil in Bordeaux, about 160 kilometres north of the Basque homeland.

Certainly whales produced oil in abundance, with over 30 tons being obtained from a single animal. The ocean itself was very productive. Although the coastline is relatively short, being only about 150 kilometres long, the sea in the Gulf of Gascony is very favourable for marine life. Water depths are fairly shallow and vary from only 50 metres at a distance of 12 kilometres from the shore, to about 200 metres 50 kilometres offshore. Shallow water and favourable currents combined to produce a rich fishery and to attract many whales.

The whaling methods used by the Basques required considerable organization. Lookouts were posted on headlands and promontories along the cost to watch for a whale blowing offshore. At a given signal, the boats set out in pursuit. One man would steer, one would carry the harpoon and five others would row. There can be little doubt that this was not an easy way to catch whales. Even after the animal died, the task was only half finished, although the dangerous part of the work was over. Then the whalers faced the long and arduous task of towing the dead carcass back to the beach where it would be cut into strips and the fat rendered into oil.

The constant slaughter near the coast gradually modified migration routes and as the whales moved offshore, the Basques built larger vessels to follow them. When it was no longer possible to tow the dead whales back to their own shoreline, the whalers processed their catch in a nearby harbour. In this way they moved up the coast to Galicia and Asturia, and possibly as far as Brittany. These longer voyages had two important effects: they stimulated a fledgling shipbuilding industry and brought the Basques into contact with Breton and other fishermen.

By the early years of the sixteenth century, they were reported to have been fishing off the coast of Ireland and had become capable of fitting out and supplying voyages of several months duration. Fishing and whaling became the most important commercial activities of the coastal region, so much so that towns along the coast incorporated whaling scenes and implements into their coats of arms.

The first voyages to Terra Nova were made around 1520 in search of cod. Following the Bretons, the Basques sailed up the west coast of Newfoundland and then north to southern Labrador, to establish whaling stations. By the middle of the century, ships were setting off for both cod and whales, but most later voyages separated the two activities. The two enterprises were indeed quite different, and it made sense to differentiate between them. Whaling, although providing greater profits, required considerably more investment in larger ships and bigger crews to man them. It was also much more risky, but the incentive for those with the capital to outfit a voyage was considerable. A single ship returning to port with a cargo of 1,000 barrels of whale oil could sell it for as much as 6,000 ducats, and this at a time when the annual salary of the Royal Auditor of Navarra was no more than 90 ducats.

Cod fishing, in contrast, was a modest enterprise, requiring less capital outlay and smaller ships. Risks were fewer and profits were correspondingly smaller. In addition to the differences in the capital investment required, however, the timing was also quite different. Fishermen going after cod could leave home early in the year, fish through the summer and be back home with their dried or salted catch by August or September. To catch migrating whales, the whaling fleet did not leave port until much later, perhaps as late as July, and did not return until the end of the year or, in some cases, much later.

Generally, the whaling ships were the largest of those that crossed the Atlantic. Most of the ships which were devoted entirely to cod fishing were of less than 100 tons, whereas the average tonnage of ships setting out for both cod and whales appears to have been about 250 tons. The single-purpose whalers were larger still, with tonnages ranging up to 700. The ships were real workhorses. Designed for seaworthiness and for carrying cargo, they were slow but safe. They were exceedingly "beamy," with the width being usually slightly more than half the length. Typically, a large galleon of between 400 and 500 tons would have been about 17 metres long and perhaps around 10 to 11 metres wide. In theory they carried 4 barrels of whale oil per ton, with each barrel holding up to 400 pounds of oil. However, this tends to overestimate their capacity, and it would have required a very large galleon of between 600 and 700 tons to transport 2,000 barrels.

Even in peacetime, whaling ships were well armed. At the end of December 1553, a burgess of the Spanish town of Orio chartered his galleon, "a french ship of about 180 tons burden called *Santa Maria*," to two merchants of Deba for the whale fishery "in Tierranoba." In the contract he agreed that it would be "ready and outfitted with all cables and anchors and masts and sails and tackle, plus 6 large iron cannon, plus 18 versos [swivel guns] with two breech chambers for each piece, and all the stone shot, and one quintal [100 pounds] of gunpowder for the artillery, and all the pikes and half pikes and lances and darts that are necessary." Each party to the contract would provide "a third each of everything necessary for the said voyage, people, provisions, barrels, arms and cauldrons, and harpoon ropes, and hawsers, and all other supplies, provisions, and munition needed."

In addition to the gunpowder mentioned earlier for the artillery pieces, each of the three merchants agreed to add "20 pounds of gunpowder for arquebusses, plus 20 gross of arrows, plus 6 dozen small darts."[1] All this armament, wielded by a crew of about forty-five, proved, however, to be insufficient because in the summer of 1554 the *Santa Maria* was captured at Los Hornos by a French force on a raiding expedition out of Butes. This has been identified as Red Bay on the Labrador coast and is still described as the best harbour in the area. Los Hornos is thought to have been near the Nelly and Lily islands and is the site of the only known battle on the coast.[2] Although it resulted in the capture of four ships, including the *Santa Maria* and lasted "one day and one night," the fighting caused few casualties.

The ship seems to have survived relatively intact. It was taken back to Red Bay by its French captors and there, by a document dated August 25, 1554, was granted outright to its captain, Domingo de Segura, "so that no one else may own a part nor have anything to do with the said ship."[3] How the original owner felt about this deal is not recorded.

Whaling in the Strait of Belle Isle was attractive not only to the merchants who outfitted the ships but also to the men who manned them and undertook the hard and dangerous work involved in getting the vessels across the ocean, catching the whales and processing the catch. Reasons for this are made clear in many of the legal documents setting out the conditions of the voyages. The crew were fed and looked after throughout the voyage and they were able to obtain provisions and shelter at no cost while they were in Labrador. However, instead of being paid wages for their work, the crew received a share of the proceeds from the catch. The following excerpt from the *Santa Maria*'s charter gives some interesting details. Joanes de Urdayde, who provided the ship, was to receive "the fourth part of all the fishing profits ... and likewise should there be some perquisite or unexpected find on the outward or homeward voyage the fourth part of any such perquisite or unexpected find." However, "the crew of the said ship should receive the third part of all the fishing, profit or unexpected find," and the remainder, with some minor exceptions, would go to the two merchants who chartered the ship.[4] Clearly this was of great advantage to the crew and provided them with considerable incentive. About fifteen years after the voyage of the *Santa Maria*, Joan Martinez de Recalde described the system of profit sharing: "There is not to be found one mariner, apprentice seaman, or ship's boy who would wish to navigate or do the said voyage in any other way; in this way they return to their homes very much more content ... than with many reales paid as regular wages."[5]

The story of the Basque voyages to North America began unfolding in the early 1970s when Selma Barkham, a self-styled expert on Basque history, began to unearth references to the Labrador coast in whaling documents stored in the Consulado archives of Burgos. Moving from one archive to another in the Basque region and then on to museums in Paris and London, she searched more than 5,000 documents to determine the locations of the Basque harbours in Terra Nova. Then, in 1977, she made a historic visit to the Labrador coast with several Canadian geographers and archaeologists. There they found ample evidence of ovens used for processing whale oil, red tiles used for covering roofs, and even a four-hundred-year-old harpoon head which was only partly buried in gravel near Schooner Cove.

In the following year they traced the wreck of a Basque galleon, the *San Juan*, which had sunk in Red Bay and which divers located in 40 feet of water only 90 feet from the shore. The location of the wreck had been discovered from legal documents held in the archives of the Spanish town of Onate. Other documents attested to the fate of the ship: "Having completed the whale fishing and being ready to return to Spain there came upon them in the said port a tempest which, after the bow moorings had been broken, stirred the ship round, and blew her ashore so that with all the cargo of whale oil she had on board, a quantity of a thousand barrels, they left her in the said Terranova, the said captain, Ramos de Arrieta, having collected all the rigging, sails, cables and supplies that he could remove with his crew, and all that they removed, the said Ramos de Arrieta took back to Spain in the ship of Joanes de Portu."[6]

Joanes had taken a half-share in the outfitting of the *San Juan*, and being keen to recover as much of his investment as possible, he returned to Red Bay in the following year when he found the ship still grounded on the shore and still containing much of its cargo. He then unloaded what could still be salvaged and sent the barrels off to France and Spain, where they were sold. To "his partner and to some of the mariners who had been in the last ship and were present again the following year he gave part of the said barrels with fair accounting, and after he had returned to Spain, from the whale oil that had been brought back and from the net profit after the costs had been paid, he shared out and gave to the mariners that which was their due."[7]

In 1977 four sites— Red Bay, Chateau Bay, West Ste. Modeste and Schooner Cove— were identified during a brief survey of the Labrador coast, and these, together with the later discovery of the *San Juan*, prompted considerable archaeological interest in the following years.

Red Bay, known to the Basques as Buttes or Buytres, was selected as the most important site, partly because of its obvious importance in the notarial documents unearthed by Selma Barkham, but also because of the apparent size of the deposits and the relatively undisturbed state in which they were found. Excavation first concentrated on Saddle Island at the mouth of the harbour. The island protects the harbour from the turbulent waters of the strait and has a low, sandy central area with two rocky headlands at either end. Most of the shore stations have been found on these headlands or opposite them on the mainland. In both areas there is good shelter from the prevailing winds, as well as fairly deep water close to the shore, a necessary prerequisite for beaching whale carcasses as close as possible to the processing works.

Work at Red Bay proceeded in much the same fashion as had already been developed and used successfully along the Basque coast in the previous centuries. The season was long, with ships arriving in the early summer to coincide with the northward migration of the right whale from the Gulf into the Strait of Belle Isle. Following their arrival at Red Bay, the galleons anchored in a sheltered spot and remained there throughout the summer, acting essentially as a kind of floating warehouse. They would leave again as soon as they were full, but if the catch of right whales was insufficient, they would remain at anchor until well into the colder weather to catch the bowhead whales, an Arctic whale which migrated south in front of the pack ice and which probably arrived in the strait in late October, remaining in that vicinity for several months.

Often the ships did not arrive back in Europe until the following January. On occasion they stayed too late and were forced by ice and bad weather to remain throughout the harsh Labrador winter. Men died, not from starvation but from scurvy, which broke out in late winter or early spring due to a lack of fresh vegetables.

As soon as the ships arrived and anchored, men set to work to repair the damage of the previous winter to the shore stations. These consisted largely of the tryworks used to process the oil. Up to half a dozen stone fireboxes, about 1.5 metres in diameter, were set in a line to hold and heat the copper cauldrons in which blubber would be

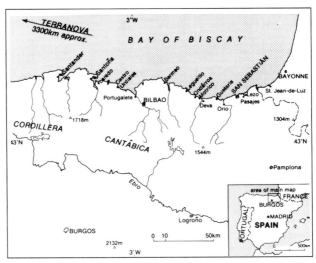

*The Basque area in the southeast corner of the Bay of Biscay. Whalers were forced to change their methods and locations when whales changed their migration routes in response to being hunted.*
(Courtesy *Canadian Geographic*)

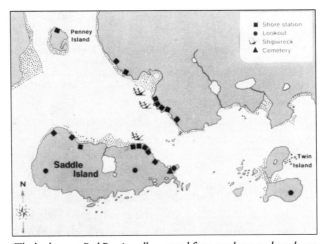

*The harbour at Red Bay is well protected from northeast and southwest winds by Saddle Island, which lies across the entrance. Deep water exists close to shore, and evidence of repeated building has been found in this area.* (Courtesy J. Tuck, Memorial University)

*Town seals of Biarritz and Motrico dating back to the Middle Ages and illustrating the importance of whaling to the Basque economy.* (Courtesy J. Tuck, Memorial University)

*Operations showing the flensing and rendering of blubber into oil, then transported by cart.*
*In* Traite des Pêches, *Vol. 11 (Paris, 1768).* (Courtesy National Archives of Canada, C-103905)

*A general view of the whale fishery. In this rather frenzied scene, the small boats, unlike those off the coast of Labrador, are being supplied by large ships sent out from the mother country.* (Courtesy National Archives of Canada, C-032707)

*Pursuit of the Greenland whale, published in* Conquest of Canada, *by G.D. Warburton (London, 1849). Although much later than the era of the Basque whalers, this wood engraving shows similar features—the use of hand-held harpoons from small boats.* (Courtesy National Archives of Canada, C-010494)

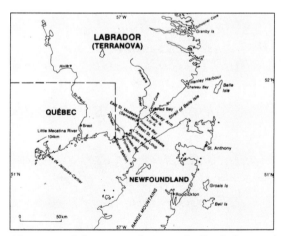

*The Basque whaling area in the Strait of Belle Isle, between the northern tip of Newfoundland and the Labrador mainland. Although Basque fishers and whalers spread out along the southern coast of Quebec and into the St. Lawrence, their major harbours were located close to the whales as they migrated through the strait.* (Courtesy *Canadian Geographic*)

melted down. Some were dug into sloping beaches and some were built on level ground, but in each case a terrace, either natural or manmade, was provided behind the cauldrons on the side farthest from the sea. This allowed the men to work the cauldrons and control the rendering process. Most of the tryworks were covered by a solid wooden structure framed with a roof made from red tiles brought out specifically for that purpose. One ship alone is known to have imported 6,000 tiles around 1560.

Men standing on the terrace tended the cauldrons, forking strips of blubber into them for rendering, and occasionally stoking up the fire, also with bits of blubber. It was undoubtedly a messy business. The blubber in the fire would crackle and explode and there are remains to show that the cauldrons themselves sometimes broke from almost continuous use throughout several seasons. Even on their first visit, the archaeologists could see the obvious remnants of charred blubber caked into the stone remains of the tryworks. Later excavations showed just how dirty the process could be by the discovery of heavy deposits of fat which had seeped far into the ground below.

Oil was removed from the cauldrons by men working with long-handled ladles who scooped the rendered oil into barrels of water where the dross would sink to the bottom while the pure oil floated to the surface. From there it was carefully ladled into barrels for storage on the anchored ships to await the long voyage home.

The hunt also followed the methods which had been perfected in the Bay of Biscay. When a whale was sighted by a lookout, small boats called *chalupas* (shallops) set out in pursuit. These were about eight metres long, and were built for speed being relatively narrow so that they could cut through the water. Built of oak, the frames were sawed from natural curves and were covered in thin planks a little more than ten millimetres thick. Above the water line these were overlapped in a clinker-built construction, but, presumably in order to provide a faster boat, the area below the water line was smooth, with the planks laid edge to edge.

Like the boats used in the Basques' home waters, they carried a crew of seven, five to row, one to steer and one with the harpoon. When they were close enough to the whale, the harpooner would drive his harpoon into its flesh as far as possible, and back off quickly. None of the shallops recovered from Red Bay were designed to have a line tied to the boat, and it is therefore probable that the men rowed after the wounded whale rather than being towed along by it. A drogue, or small sea anchor, attached to the harpoon would slow the whale down, and as it tired and surfaced more often to breathe, other harpoons with drogues would be set in place. Eventually, as the whale lost blood and became exhausted, the boats would row close and a long knife was thrust in, seeking some vital part. When the animal was finally dead, there remained the long, tiring job of towing it back to shore. At the processing works, the tail and the flippers were cut off to make it easier to rotate the floating carcass, which was then dismembered with the blubber being cut, first into long strips and then into smaller pieces to fit the cauldron.

All this activity required hundreds, if not thousands of casks and barrels. Most ships would bring the casks with them from Europe, but to save space on the outward voyage, these would be loaded in the form of pre-cut staves ready for assembly in Terra Nova. Consequently, ships always took with them a cooper, or barrel maker, and ample evidence of cooperages is available at Red Bay. So far, all the cooperages have been found on elevated terraces above the tryworks. For obvious reasons the sites were chosen so that prevailing winds would blow the smoke and smell of the rendering away from the coopers.

The coopers were an important part of the enterprise, because if the casks were faulty, the precious oil would leak away and with it would go the owners' profits. Cooperages were substantial structures with tiled roofs like those of the tryworks.

It is not yet clear whether the tryworks were fully enclosed, but the cooperages certainly were. Walls kept out the wind and the rain, and, unlike most of the other men, the coopers lived in their workshops. Small hearths have been found, together with personal items used for food and drink. From the remains of tools which have been unearthed, it seems that the coopers were capable of performing all the work needed to completely build a barrel starting from raw lumber.

Although this probably was rarely done, repair and maintenance of the barrels required a capability in every aspect of the work. Adzes for hollowing out the inside of staves, as well as knives for finishing off the outside, have been located. Tools to cut the groove into which the top of the cask would fit are among the most common artifact discovered, but heavy wedges to split wood into staves and iron blades from large planes are also present. The staves were held tightly together with wooden hoops, and fragments of tools to set them in place have been found inside the remains of the cooperages.

While the coopers lived in their workshops and the officers stayed on the ship, the hunters and the men in the processing works lived much more spartan lives. It seems that they were generally left to fend for themselves. They lived where they could, finding a secluded spot well away from the tryworks so that they would be less bothered by the smell and the smoke. Often their meagre dwellings would incorporate a convenient feature of the landscape which might provide some protection from the elements. Occasionally a dwelling has been found where a crack in the bedrock might provide a natural fireplace. At one site on Saddle Island, a low wall had been set up beside a steep bank and the space between covered in rough local lumber. Sailcloth may have been used as a cover, but in other cases, there is evidence of roofs being constructed from poles laid close together and covered with sods and strips of baleen.

The men who rendered the blubber probably used the sites closest to the tryworks, whereas those sites farther away are more likely to have been used by the men who took part in the hunt. There was no need for them to be close to the shore station, and in addition to a place to live, they needed a beach, not too far from the position where their lookout was posted, from which to launch their boats. None of these dwellings seem to have been very substantial, compared with the cooperages or the tryworks which were used year after year.

Although food was provided during the voyage, when they got to Labrador the men had to obtain most of their sustenance by themselves. This was not a great hardship with the availability of whale meat, fish, and local game. Codfish, capelin and probably salmon, along with birds, such as the Great Auk, were undoubtedly part of their diet. Seal bones and the remains of polar bears have been found in various sites. The ships carried wine and cider, and berries would have been plentiful at the end of summer. Hunger was not much of a problem, but the protein-rich diet provided no protection against scurvy if the ships were forced to winter in the strait.

The work was hard and could be extremely dangerous. Accidents must have happened. Small boats would capsize, and there was the ever-present danger of serious injury. In 1982 a burial ground was found at the southern end of Saddle Island. This was excavated over the next four years to reveal 60 graves containing the remains of more than 140 whalers. About half of the graves contained a single skeleton, while the others held two or more individuals. Some show evidence of a real disaster. One contained the decayed bodies of 12 or 13 individuals who had been buried with little ceremony in a large shallow pit. Possibly they died during the winter when the weather and hard ground made a proper funeral impossible. Another grave contained the remains of 7 whalers who had obviously been buried at the same time, and it has been surmised that this was the disastrous results of a small boat (carrying 7 men) capsizing during a hunt.

Men who died in accidents probably succumbed quickly to their injuries, but those who fell victim to disease sometimes had the opportunity to make some preparation for their death. Two wills are known to have survived from this era. These are the earliest wills drawn up in North America, and although both are quite legal, they were drawn up without the help of a notary. Indeed, this lack may have been a concern to the men who risked their lives in this barbarous land, and witnesses to both wills complain about, and testify to, the absence of any proper legal amenities. "Neither on the said ship nor in the said port was there a royal notary or one of the number in the said town nor is there a notary in the province of Terranoba since it is a land of savages, and thus the said master Joanes de Arriaga, surgeon wrote it."[8] The will referred to was that of a young man barely twenty years of age who dictated it at midnight on Christmas Eve, 1584, in Red Bay. Joanes de Echaniz, from the Spanish town of Orio, made the forlorn request that his body be taken home for burial, but knowing that this would likely be impossible, he sent money, such as he had, back to Spain for "the offices and obsequies of the burial day." Apart from a pound of wax for "our lady of Aizarnazabal" and about nine reals for religious observances, Echaniz bequeathed all his worldly goods to his wife and daughter.[9] Only three witnesses were available to testify to the will "because it was midnight and some of the sailors of the said ship were working on land rendering whales to make train oil and the others were sleeping on board ship exhausted due to sheer work."[10]

One of the first group of bodies found during the excavations were those of men who had, perhaps, been the last to die. Twelve skeletons were discovered placed carefully in two rows but, apparently, never buried. They had been laid out on the earth floor of a simple dwelling which seems to have once housed the crew from one of the shallops. There they remained throughout the centuries until the surrounding vegetation crept back to reclaim the area. Although the reasons for their unusual "burial" are not clear, the most obvious explanation is that their deaths occurred at the end of the whaling era. Probably they were laid out during the winter when frozen ground made it impossible to dig a grave and shortly before the ships left, with the intention, which was never realized, of returning the following year.

Estimates, based primarily on the legal documents from French and Spanish archives, indicate that the whaling era along the Labrador shore lasted for at least half a century. At its height, as many as twenty ships might have been active in the Strait of Belle Isle, although nine or ten is the more probable number for most years. In 1554, however, it is known that there were sixteen or seventeen ships based in the harbour at Red Bay. Estimates of the total catch over that period of time range as high as 20,000, and the Basques' very success may have contributed to their undoing. Whales breed slowly, usually only one calf per year, and a hunt which took even 10,000 over a fifty-year period could have seriously depleted the stocks or forced a major change in migration patterns. Certainly today, few, if any, right or bowhead whales pass through the strait. Bowheads are now confined to the Arctic regions, while a small group of right whales spend the summer in the Bay of Fundy and the Gulf of Maine.

But the end of Basque whaling along the Labrador coast was not caused only by a lack of whales. After about fifteen years of relative peace in Terra Nova, there are indications in parish records of hostilities with the indigenous population. Privateering by the French, Dutch and English became prevalent in mid-century, and from 1575, there are reports of the smaller codfish ships being attacked by privateers.

The Basques themselves were not blameless, however, and in the mid-1550s there are numerous references to Basque ships indulging in privateering expeditions. This upsurge of licensed pirates in the last quarter of the century may have had little effect on the larger galleons which were well able to defend themselves, but it certainly must have made their owners somewhat nervous. These ships, however, became unavailable for whaling expeditions when they were withdrawn from their commercial activities to sail with the ill-fated Spanish Armada in 1588. Thereafter, with the finances of the Spanish crown severely depleted, private capital seems to have become insufficient and this, coupled with a probable depletion in the number of whales, seems to have been enough to close down the enterprise altogether.

From being entirely independent around Labrador in the sixteenth century, Basque whalers moved into the North Atlantic, where they not only fished for themselves but also helped to establish whaling activities for other nations in the early years of the seventeenth century. In 1611 an English company employed "sixe Biscaines for the killing of the whale" in one of the first English ventures to Spitzbergen.[11] Knowing little of the art themselves, the English were careful to treat the Basques "very kindly and friendly during this their first voyage" so that they could learn the "business of striking the whale, as well as they."[12] Around the same time, King James I wrote to the King of Spain for permission to employ Basques as harpooners, and twenty-four are known to have been in the Spitzbergen area in 1613.

In a treaty of 1619, Holland, England and Denmark carved up the shores around Spitzbergen for their exclusive use, and the Basques were then unable to process oil in their usual shore stations. They responded by developing a method which allowed them to render oil on board ship—the first-known factory ships. This permitted them to continue fishing for some time, but both whaling and cod fishing declined significantly throughout the eighteenth century.

The date of their final departure from the shores of Labrador is still not known, and as late as 1636, a French Jesuit priest from Newfoundland wrote home with an account which stated that the whaling around Newfoundland waters was still dominated by the Basques.

CHAPTER SEVEN

# *T*HE LATER YEARS

*O*f the various explorations described in this book, three had little to do with subsequent discoveries in North America and were hardly more than interludes in the opening up of the Canadian land mass. Brendan's epic journey, if indeed it ever took place, left few traces other than in Irish folk memories. Similarly, the Viking explorations of Vinland and the establishment of Basque whaling stations in Labrador contributed nothing (as far as is known) to later voyages. Knowledge of both was lost and forgotten for many centuries until recent archaeological work provided evidence that they had actually occurred. Only Cabot's rather vague voyage of 1497, which was followed in 1583 by Gilbert, and Cartier's explorations of the Gulf of St. Lawrence in the 1540s set the scene for further developments.

Cabot's voyage eventually led directly to the English search for a northwest passage. Admittedly, this took some time to gain momentum, but after Frobisher's three expeditions between 1576 and 1578, there was almost continuous excitement for the next forty years. John Davis made three separate trips to the area west of Greenland between 1585 and 1587. He sailed up the Greenland coast, reaching as far north as latitude 72°, explored both sides of the strait which now bears his name, and discovered and explored Cumberland Sound in Baffin Island. On his return to England after the third voyage, he wrote and published his book, *The Worldes Hydrographical Description*, giving further impetus to the search for the passage.[1]

By 1602, the East India Company had become interested and sent out navigator George Weymouth to follow up Davis's work in "the good and luckie ship called *Discovery*." The ship may have been lucky, but Weymouth was not.[2] He appears to have discovered little, if anything, that was not known to Frobisher and Davis and was forced to turn home when his crew mutinied. At this time there was a hiatus in English exploration, and the next voyage from the British Isles did not take place until 1606. Before then, however, the Danes, under Christian IV, sent out three separate expeditions, trying, primarily, to make contact with the lost Icelandic colonies in Greenland. Their expeditions proved largely fruitless, but one of the leaders, John Knight, an Englishman, found employment with the Muscovy Company when he returned to England. His voyage with them almost resulted in the loss of his ship during a severe storm, and he was only able to limp home after extensive repairs. The Muscovy Company, however, did not give up and now employed Henry Hudson. In 1607 and 1608, he twice sailed northeast looking for a passage beyond Russia. Both expeditions failed because of the cold and the heavy ice, but Hudson penetrated as far north as latitude 81° to Spitzbergen. His later accounts of the abundant whales he saw stimulated the North Atlantic whaling industry there. As recounted in the previous chapter, the Basque whalers found employment when the supply of whales decreased in the Strait of Belle Isle.

The Muscovy Company had now financed three unsuccessful expeditions in three years and were unwilling to throw good money after bad. However, the Dutch East India Company based in Amsterdam took up the torch and hired Hudson to make another attempt. In this, his third voyage, he again travelled north and east, attempting to pass the island of Novaya Zemlya, which separates the Barents and Kara seas between 70°N and 80°N. His crew, however, had other ideas: they mutinied and refused to allow him to proceed.

On his return, he was able to persuade them to sail west in more temperate, lower latitudes, and in doing so, they sailed across the Atlantic to Newfoundland, Nova Scotia and the coast of Maine. This was one of the longest voyages of the time, but its primary effect had little to do with the northern regions. Towards the end of the voyage, he discovered and entered the Hudson River, one of the three water routes into North America. This was sufficient reason for the Dutch to claim the area, and in 1614, only five years after his voyage, they founded the colony of New Amsterdam—present-day New York.

Hudson's three attempts to pass through the ice-filled waters of the Barents Sea led him to switch his interest from east to west, and he decided that it was more worthwhile to look for a northwest passage. England was again ready to support another attempt, and his last voyage began in April 1610 with renewed English support. This was the voyage which, more than anything, left his name firmly fixed on the map.[3] His specific instructions were to try to find a passage "to the ocean called the South Sea" by examining the various gulfs which "Davis saw, but durst not enter." Leaving England on April 17, he sailed to Iceland, around the tip of Greenland and up the Davis Strait. By the end of June he had found Hudson Strait and by the late fall he had traversed Hudson Bay south to James Bay. There he decided to spend the winter.

Rations were short, the winter was hard and only about two weeks' supply of food was left when the ship broke free of ice on June 4 the following year. On June 22 his crew mutinied to prevent further exploration. Hudson was seized and, together with his son and six others, was cast adrift in a small boat. They were never heard of again. Only eight of the mutineers managed to get back to London, but they brought with them news of the great discovery; a navigable strait leading into open water which gave every impression of a free passage to the East.

Although condemned to death, the mutineers were all allowed to go free, probably because they were the only living souls with first-hand knowledge of the bay. Indeed, some accompanied the next voyage, which, under Thomas Button, charted the west coast of Hudson Bay and showed that no entrance to the East could be gained there.

Hudson's discovery had raised so much hope in England that the North-West Company was formed in 1612 with a royal charter giving the founders a monopoly of any passage discovered in the vicinity of Hudson Bay. Button's expedition had been sent off by some of the founding members before the charter had been obtained, but his return in 1613, with the bad news that the bay was closed on the western side, did not diminish the company's ardour. In 1614, his

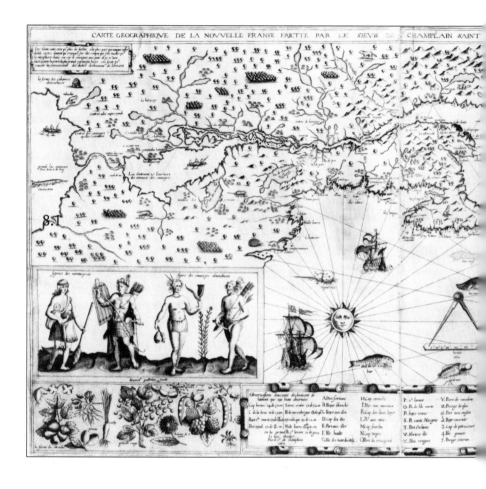

Woodcut showing Jens Munk's meetings with Inuit on the north shore of Hudson Strait in 1619. Munk anchored at two places in the strait, both depicted here. Published in Munk's account of the voyage in Navigatio Septrionalis (Copenhagen, 1624). (Courtesy Det Kongelige Bibliothek, Copenhagen)

*Champlain's map of the St. Lawrence area, 1612. This map was drawn for navigators who sailed with uncorrected French compasses and is the first reasonably accurate map of the St. Lawrence River and the Atlantic coastline.* (Courtesy National Library of Canada)

*Munk secured his ships for the winter at Port Churchill, in Hudson Bay. The men lived on the ships, and with no fresh vegetables, most of them died of scurvy by spring. Published in* Navigatio Septrionalis *(Copenhagen, 1624).* (Courtesy Det Kongelige Bibliothek, Copenhagen)

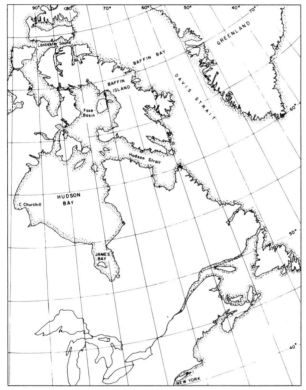

*General map of northeast Canada showing where explorers searched for the northwest passage.* (Drawing by Terry Dyer)

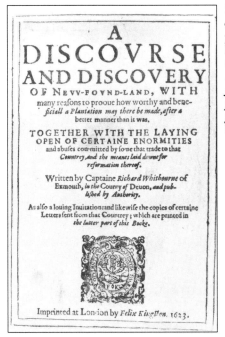

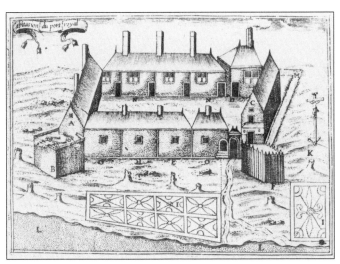

*Champlain's settlement at Port Royal. Although the plan is thought to be accurate, the picture itself is largely fanciful.* (Courtesy The Champlain Society)

cousin, Captain William Gibbons, sailed for the company but could not penetrate into the Hudson Strait because of heavy ice.

Further expeditions, in 1615 and 1616, were mounted to search for the passage. In both of these, Robert Bylot was the captain and William Baffin, the pilot. These voyages showed that there was no way through to the East, at least no way that could be navigated with sailing ships. During the second voyage, Baffin piloted them north to 75°, carefully mapping the region. They coasted up the eastern side of Baffin Island and discovered Lancaster Sound, which Baffin named but did not recognize as the only viable passage in this region.

On their return they were convinced that no passage existed. Their conviction spread, and English interest ceased for fifteen years before it was briefly revived by Foxe and James. Both sailed to Hudson Bay in 1631 but achieved little of note, although their names are still remembered, having been given to Foxe Basin and James Bay.

Although England had lost interest in the passage, her voyages through the northern ice had served to reawaken the enthusiasm of the Danes. Christian's early attempts to regain contact with his former colony in Greenland had been unsuccessful, but now, in 1619, he fitted two ships, perhaps to try again, but primarily to see if the Danes could succeed where England had failed. This was one of the worst voyages of the period, and although extreme, the conditions they experienced were not atypical.

Command was given to Jens Munk with two ships and a crew of 65. They sailed from Denmark on May 16, 1619, and landed at Churchill in Hudson Bay in September where they set up for the winter.

Initially, everything went well. Provisions were adequate, game was available, and beer and wine could be had relatively freely. However, scurvy set in shortly after the New Year. By January 21, thirteen of the crew were sick, and by the end of February, about a third of the original complement were dead. By April the number of deaths had doubled, and only four men were not completely bedridden. Quickly the others succumbed, and by June 4 only four were still alive. Fortunately, perhaps, they were driven from their beds by the stench of death in the ship and struggled to the shore. There, one more died, but the remaining three gradually regained their strength by eating whatever fresh fish and greenery they could lay their hands on. By July they had recovered to the extent that they were able to get the smaller of the two ships under way and to manoeuvre it, by September, back to Bergen, Norway. This disaster effectively halted all further Danish exploration of a northwest passage.

There is, of course, a northwest passage through Lancaster Sound north of Baffin Island, but it would not be traversed until a twentieth-century icebreaker made the trip in the 1970s. At these high latitudes it was impossible for the small sailing ships of the sixteenth or seventeenth century to get through.

Nevertheless, a considerable amount had been learned from the search. Davis Strait and Baffin Bay had been explored up to latitude 75°N, and the three great sea routes into the interior—the St. Lawrence, the Hudson River and Hudson Bay—had been opened up. Furthermore, not only had no northwest passage been found, it had been accepted that no northwest passage existed, and this turned men's minds to other matters.

When it became obvious that the new lands discovered on the far side of the Atlantic were not only not part of Asia, but provided no access through to Asia, some use had to be found for them, particularly if England and France were to compete with Spain and her valuable possessions in the south.

Colonization came to mind, but it would be wrong to suggest that it was only the failure of finding a passage to the East that gave rise to this. In England the two ideas had existed side by side ever since Cabot had returned from his great discovery, and Gilbert's "possession" of Newfoundland in 1583 was the first English step in that direction. France, on the other hand, had shown little interest in the northwest passage, although Cartier started out looking for it on his first voyage, but the instructions for his third voyage concentrated instead on settlement and exploration for mineral wealth. However, his half-hearted attempt to settle the St. Lawrence area failed completely, and for half a generation his countrymen were occupied in internal turmoil and had little time to devote to overseas exploration.

France's first proper attempt at colonization occurred in 1562 when two ships set off from Le Havre bound for Florida. The colonists lasted less than a year before they were forced to abandon the site. Another attempt in 1564 in the same area also led to failure, and further efforts were put off until the end of the century. By that time, fur traders were active in the St. Lawrence, and one of these, Pierre Chauvin, made an abortive attempt in 1600 to start a colony at Tadoussac, about two hundred kilometres downstream from Quebec. This also failed, and it was not until Samuel de Champlain made an alliance with the Algonquin Indians at Tadoussac, in 1603, that the settlers had any hope of lasting through the severe Canadian winter. In that year Champlain had journeyed to the St. Lawrence primarily to scout out the area with a view to colonization. By the time he returned to France, he was convinced that settlement would be both useful and possible.

His first attempt at colonization, however, was in the Bay of Fundy, where, in 1604, he founded a settlement at St. Croix Island. In the following year the settlers moved across the bay to Port Royal, where they managed reasonably well, being displaced only when a British force from Virginia attacked them in 1613.

With the founding of Quebec City in 1608, Champlain set France on the road to success. The colony suffered a terrible first winter, but was relieved by another expedition which arrived in the following spring. From then on, it gradually gained strength. Champlain explored upriver and, by 1611, was on the site of Montreal, where he set up fortifications and named them Place Royal. French traders soon spread throughout Quebec and Ontario, travelling the lengths of Lake Huron, Erie and Ontario and navigating up the principal rivers of Quebec. The fur trade blossomed, cash benefits accumulated, and France's infant colony grew, not without hardship and struggles, to become New France and one of the founding nations of Canada.

While France was busy developing the basin of the St. Lawrence River, English interest was centred elsewhere. Colonial ventures really started with Sir Humphrey Gilbert's annexation of St. John's harbour and its environs in 1583, although there were few, if any, changes to the area as a result. His claim of English sovereignty was virtually ignored by other countries using the harbour, and the international fishery in the area continued essentially as it had before his arrival.

Nevertheless, other European nations did not dispute the claim, and English fishermen began to fish the Grand Banks in ever-increasing numbers.[4] Soon the fishery "became the stay and support of the West Countries," bringing in £100,000 annually and providing employment for great numbers of "catchers on boats and curers on land." However, there was no rush to settle Newfoundland and, indeed, the initial attempts to found a colony were met with great resistance. West Country merchants, who had established a monopoly in the fish trade, had no wish to see colonial competition, and preferred "that Newfoundland should always be considered as a great English ship, moored near to the banks, during the fishing season for the convenience of English fishermen."[5]

This reluctance to settle on the somewhat inhospitable shores of Newfoundland did not, however, extend to more temperate areas. Although Gilbert's voyage showed no immediate profits, his early proselytizing and his eager enthusiasm for colonization spurred others to follow in his footsteps. When he drowned on his way back to England, his charter from Elizabeth, giving him the right to settle areas outside Christian influence, had only one year left to run. On its expiry, it was renewed by his half-brother, Sir Walter Raleigh, who immediately sent out ships with the intention of looking for land to settle in the area which had become known as Virginia, in honour of the virgin queen, Elizabeth.

His captains brought back encouraging reports of Roanoke Island, and the first colonists were shipped out in 1585. Landing among unfriendly Indians and making little or no attempt to grow their own food, they quickly ran out of provisions. Indeed, they would almost certainly have perished had Sir Francis Drake not passed by on his way home from the West Indies and offered to take them back to England. Another attempt was made in 1587, but communication with England was cut off by the outbreak of war with Spain, and when these were re-established again in 1590, the second group of colonists had vanished almost without trace.

Although led by Sir Richard Grenville, the driving force in these ventures was Raleigh. Despite enormous costs and many setbacks, Raleigh persevered, realizing that the planting of colonies was, as Sir

Francis Bacon said, like the planting of trees: "You must make account to lose almost twenty years profit, and expect your recompence in the end."[6]

Not until 1607 did the English achieve success when Jamestown, Virginia, was settled. By then the war with Spain was over and money which had been tied up in outfitting warships, and privateers could now be redirected towards colonial investments. Interest also developed, once again, in Newfoundland.

Only three years after the colonization of Jamestown, Gilbert's act of possession was turned into fact when the newly formed Newfoundland Company obtained a charter from James I to colonize the southeastern part of the island, the express purpose being to "receive and make safe the said trade of Fishing to our subjectes forever," although there was, in addition, the intention to "make some commendable benefit for the use of mankynde by the landes and proffittes thereof."[7]

In August 1610, thirty-nine men landed with their leader, John Guy, in Cupids Cove on the Avalon Peninsula. Other colonies followed. Two years later the English were in Bermuda, and during the next twenty years, the British Empire was well established.

The early voyages of Cabot and Cartier had at last borne fruit. Settlement flourished and expanded. Crossing the Atlantic with ever-increasing frequency, the number of French and English settlers grew with each decade. Traditional rivalries made the journey to the new colonies as easily as did the colonists themselves, and settlers could not and did not want to avoid being caught up in wars which had their origins in Europe. Much of the early colonial history of Canada is a record of fights and skirmishes for land and fishing rights, but in time the traditional rivalries gave way to peaceful co-existence. The various colonies grew to have more in common with each other than with the mother country, and with this realization, the transition to an independent Canada became a fairly natural progression.

# NOTES AND SOURCES

## INTRODUCTION

1. Gaspar Correa, "Lendas da India," *The Three Voyages of Vasco da Gama,* 1st series, XLII, Hakluyt Society, 1896, p. 331.
2. C.R. Markham, ed., *The Journal of Christopher Columbus During his First Voyage, 1492-3,* 1st series, LXXXVI, Hakluyt Society, 1893, p. 3.
3. D. O'Sullivan, *The Age of Discovery—1400-1500,* London, Longmans, 1984.
4. J.R. Hale, *Renaissance Exploration,* New York, W.W. Norton and Co., 1968.
5. F.G. Davenport, ed., *European Treaties Bearing upon the History of the United States,* Carnegie Institution of Washington, publication no. 254, Gloucester, Peter Smith, 1967, p. 95.
6. H.C. Field, ed., *Dawn of Empire,* No. 2 of *The British Empire,* New York, Time-Life Books, 1972.

### Other Sources

Cipolla, C.M. *Guns and Sails in the Early Phase of European Expansion, 1400-1700.* London: Collins, 1966.

Cohen, J.M., ed. *The Four Voyages of Christopher Columbus.* London: Penguin, 1969.

Penrose, B. *Travel and Discovery in the Renaissance.* Boston: Harvard University Press, 1960.

Unger, R.W. *The Ship in the Medieval Economy, 600-1600.* London: Croom Helm, 1980.

Waters, D.W. *The Art of Navigation in England in Elizabethan and Early Stuart Times.* Hartford: Yale University Press, 1958.

Waugh, Teresa, trans. *The Travels of Marco Polo.* London: Sidgwick and Jackson, 1984.

## CHAPTER ONE—ST. BRENDAN AND THE IRISH

1. J.J. O'Meara, trans., *The Voyage of Saint Brendan,* Dolmen Press, 1978. Quotations relating to Brendan's voyage are taken from this source except where noted.
2. G. Ashe, *Land to the West,* New York, Viking Press, 1962.
3. K. Meyer, trans., *Voyage of Bran,* London, David Nutt, 1895, p. 97.
4. H.P.A. Oskamp, trans., *Voyage of Mael Duin,* Groningen, Wolters-Noordhoff, 1970, from Immran curaig Mael Duin, in the *Yellow Book of Lecan,* Trinity College, Dublin.
5. J.A. Williamson, *The Voyages of John and Sebastian Cabot,* published for the London Historical Association, London, G. Bell, 1937.
6. Dicuil, *Liber de Mensura Orbis Terrae,* J.J. Tierney, ed., Dublin Institution for Advanced Studies, 1967. (Latin and English text).
7. W. Stokes, *Lives of the Saints from the Book of Lismore,* Oxford, Oxford and Clarendon Press, 1890.
8. *Liber de Mensura Orbis Terrae.*
9. Tim Severin, *The Brendan Voyage,* London, Hutchinson, 1978.
10. *Ibid.*
11. *Ibid.*
12. R. McGhee and J. Tuck, "Did the Medieval Irish Visit Newfoundland?" *Canadian Geographic,* June/July 1977.

**Other Sources**
Severin, Tim. "The Voyage of Brendan." *National Geographic,* December 1977.
———. "Voyages in a Leather Boat." *Geographical Magazine,* January 1978.

## CHAPTER TWO—THE VIKING EXPLOSION

1. A. Savage, *The Anglo-Saxon Chronicles,* Dorset Press, 1983, pp. 73-76.

**Other Sources**
Ashe, G., T. Heyerdahl, H. Ingstad, J.V. Luce, B.J. Meggers and B.L. Wallace. *The Quest for America.* London: Pall Mall, 1971.
Guralnick, E., ed. *Vikings in the West.* Archaeological Institute of America, April 1982.
Horwood, J. *Viking Discovery—L'Anse aux Meadows.* St. John's: Jesperson Press, 1985.
Ingstad, H. *Land Under the Pole Star.* London: St. Martin's Press, 1966.
———. *Westward to Vinland.* London: Jonathan Cape, 1969.
Jones, G. *The Norse Atlantic Saga.* London: Oxford University Press, 1986.

Lindsay, C. "Was L'Anse aux Meadows a Norse Outpost?" *Canadian Geographic,* February/March 1977.

Magnusson, M. *The Vikings.* London: Bodley Head, BBC, 1980.

Tuck, J. "The Norse in Newfoundland." *Canadian Collector,* March/April 1975.

Wallace, B. "The Norse in Newfoundland." *Conservation Canada,* 1977.

## CHAPTER THREE—JOHN CABOT AND THE MEN OF BRISTOL

1. Letter from Pedro de Ayala to Ferdinand and Isabella, London, July 25, 1498, Spanish Archives, Simancas.
2. The "Paris" map, *c.* 1490-1493, Paris, Bibliothèque Nationale, Section de Geographie NAW, I, pl. 13, p. 480.
3. *The European Reconnaissance,* New York, Harper Torch Books, 1968, p. 280.
4. British Museum, Cotton MSS, Vitellius, C. VII, f. 329-45. See also Hakluyt, Richard, *The Principal Navigations Voyages Traffiques and Discoveries of the English Nation, 1589-1600,* New York, AMS Press Inc., 1965, Vol. VII, p. 155.
5. John Cabot's Letters Patents, Public Record Office, Treaty Roll 178, membr. 8. See also *The Principal Navigations,* Vol. VII, pp. 139-144.
6. J.A. Williamson, *The Cabot Voyages and Bristol Discovery Under Henry VII,* published for the Hakluyt Society, Cambridge University Press, 1962, p. 33.
7. Letter from Pedro de Ayala etc., 1498.
8. Letter from John Day.
9. *Ibid.*
10. British Museum MSS 7099. See also Public Record Office Privy Seals, 13 Hen VII, December and warrants for issue 13 Hen VII, E 404, Bundle 82.
11. Calendar of State Papers, Milan, Vol. I, No. 552: J.H. Parry, ed., *The European Reconnaissance,* New York, Harper, 1968, p. 280.
12. Patent granted by Ferdinand and Isabella to Alonso de Hojeda on June 8, 1501, Spanish Archives, Simancas.
13. Grant of Pensions to Francisco Fernandez and Joao Gonsalvez, September 26, 1502, Public Record Office, London, Warrants for issue E. 404, 84/1.
14. "Chronicle of Robert Fabian," recorded in *The Principal Navigations,* Vol. VII, p. 155.
15. Letters Patent granted by Henry VII on March 19, 1501, Public Record

Office, Patent roll 16 Hen VII, pt. 1 membr 20, 21: also warrants for Privy Seals, Series II No. 216.

16. *The Cabot Voyages,* p. 134-140.

**Other Sources**

Biggar, H.P. *The Precursors of Jacques Cartier, 1497-1534—A Collection of Documents Relating to the Early History of the Dominion of Canada.* Ottawa: Public Archives of Canada. No. 5, 1911.

O'Dea, F. "Cabot's Landfall—Yet Again." *Aspects,* Newfoundland Historical Society, Vol. 4, No. 2, December 1971.

Quinn, D.B. *North America from Earliest Discovery to First Settlement.* New York: Harper and Row, 1975.

Rowe, F.W. *History of Newfoundland and Labrador.* Toronto: McGraw-Hill Ryerson, 1980.

Williamson, J.A. *The Voyages of the Cabots and the English Dictionary of North America under Henry.* Argonault Press, 1929.

## CHAPTER FOUR—THE FIRST FRENCH EXPEDITIONS

1. J.B. Brebner, *The Explorers of North America, 1492-1806,* Ohio, World Publishing Co., 1933.

2. S. Leacock, *The Mariner of St. Malo,* Glasgow, Toronto, Brook and Co., 1915.

3. R. Hakluyt, *The Principal Navigations Voyages Traffiques and Discoveries of the English Nation, 1589-1600,* New York, AMS Press Inc., 1965. (Except for the third voyage, Cartier's records are available in the original French. However, the account of his first voyage was lost for over three hundred years and was only rediscovered in Paris in the late 1800s. During this time its contents were familiar to English readers through the translation which appeared in Hakluyt's *Principal Navigations.* Quotations throughout this chapter have been taken from the *Voyages* except where otherwise noted.)

4. *The Mariner of St. Malo.*

5. M. Ross, *The Globe and Mail,* October 13, 1990.

**Other Sources**

Biggar, H.P. *A Collection of Documents Relating to Jacques Cartier and the Sieur de Roberval.* Ottawa: Public Archives of Canada, 1930.

———, trans. *The Voyages of Jacques Cartier.* Ottawa: Public Archives of Canada, F.A. Acland, 1924.

## CHAPTER FIVE—THE ELIZABETHAN THRUST

1. Richard Hakluyt, *The Principal Navigations Voyages Traffiques and Discoveries of the English Nation,* New York, AMS Press Inc., 1965. Vol. VIII, p. 34-77.
2. W.G. Hoskins, *The Age of Plunder,* London, Longmans, 1976.
3. *The Principal Navigations,* Vol. VII, p. 282.
4. "The Voyages and Colonising Enterprises of Sir Humphrey Gilbert," a collection of documents with an introduction by D.B. Quinn, Hakluyt Society, 2nd. series, Vol. LXXIII-IV, p. 17.
5. *Ibid.,* pp. 129-165.
6. *Ibid.,* pp. 170-180.
7. *Ibid.,* pp. 188-194.
8. *Ibid.,* p. 348.
9. *The Principal Navigations,* Vol. VIII, pp. 34-77.
10. Raleigh and Roanoke—Catalogue of the British Library Exhibit Hosted by the North Carolina Museum of History, 1985.
11. *The Principal Navigations,* Vol. XII, pp. 1-11, p. 85.

Parts of this chapter were originally written for *American History Illustrated* and *British Heritage.* These parts are reprinted here courtesy of the publisher, Cowles Magazines Inc.

## CHAPTER SIX—THE BASQUE WHALERS

1. Charter Party for the *Santa Maria,* 29 December, 1553. Archivo de la Real Chancilleria, Valladolid, Pleitos civiles, Taboada Olvidados, legajo 218-6.
2. Selma Barkham, "Documentary Evidence for 16th Century Basque Whaling Ships in the Strait of Belle Isle, "in *Early European Settlement and Exploitation in Atlantic Canada,* G.M. Story, ed., Selected Papers, St. John's, Memorial University, 1982.
3. Grant of the *Santa Maria* by her captors to Domingo de Segura in Red Bay, 25 August 1554. Archivo de la Real Chancilleria, Valladolid, Pleitos civiles, Moreno fenecidos, 25.
4. Charter Party for the *Santa Maria.*
5. Archivo General de Simancas, Guerra Antigua, legajo 75.
6. Selections from Testimony about the wreck of the *San Juan* in Red Bay, 1565, Archivo de la Real Chancilleria, Valladolid-Wals fenecidos, legajo 31, caja 160-1.

7. *Ibid.*

8. Testimony regarding the validity of the will of Joanes de Echaniz, Archivo Historico Provincial de Guipuzcoa, Onate, partido de San Sebastian, legajo 1808, f. 44-44v.

9. Last Will of Joanes de Echaniz written in Carrol's Cove, Labrador, 24 December 1584, Archivo Historico Provincial de Guipuzcoa, Onate, Partido de San Sebastian, legajo 1808, f. 46-47.

10. Testimony regarding the validity of the will of Joanes de Echaniz.

11. Samuel Purchas, *Purchas his Pilgrimes,* Glasgow, Glasgow University Press, 1925, Vol. 13, p. 12.

12. J.T. Jenkins, *A History of the Whale Fisheries from the Basque Fisheries of the Tenth Century to the Hunting of the Finner Whale at the Present Time,* 2nd edition, London, 1971.

Translation of the Basque documents in Notes 1 and 3-10 are given as an appendix in Barkham, Note 2.

**Other Sources**

Barkham, Selma. *The Basque Coast of Newfoundland.* Great Northern Peninsula Development Corp. Nfld., 1989.

————. "The Basque: Filling a Gap in Our History between Jacques Cartier and Champlain." *Canadian Geographic,* February/March 1978.

Douglas, W.A., and J. Bilbao. *Amarikanuak—Basques in the New World.* Reno: University of Nevada Press, 1975.

Hoyt, E. *The Whales of Canada.* Camden East: Camden House, 1984.

Quinn, D.B. "Newfoundland in the Consciousness of Europe in the Sixteenth and Early Seventeenth Centuries," in *European Settlement and Exploitation in Atlantic Canada.* G.M. Story, ed., Selected Papers, Memorial University, 1982.

Thurston, H. "The Basque Connection." *Equinox,* December 1983.

Tuck, J.A., and R. Grenier. *Red Bay Labrador—World Whaling Capital AD 1550-1600.* St. John's: Atlantic Archaeology Ltd., 1989.

————. "A Sixteenth Century Whaling Station at Red Bay Labrador," in *European Settlement and Exploitation in Atlantic Canada.* G.M. Story, ed., Selected Papers, St. John's: Memorial University, 1982.

## CHAPTER SEVEN—THE LATER YEARS

1. *The Worldes Hydrographical Description,* by John Davis, was published after his third voyage, in London in 1595. Davis made no further voyages

to the North. He sailed with naval expeditions in 1596 and 1597 and followed this with three voyages to the Far East, being killed by Japanese pirates on the last trip.

2. Samuel Purchas, *Purchas his Pilgrimes,* Glasgow, Glasgow University Press, 1925, see Vol. XIV, pp. 306-318.

3. *Ibid.* Vol. XIII, pp. 294-412.

4, 5. Good descriptions of the growth of the Newfoundland fishery are provided in *History of Newfoundland,* by D.W. Prowse, London, Macmillan, 1895, and F.W. Rowe, in the more recent book *A History of Newfoundland and Labrador,* Toronto, McGraw-Hill Ryerson, 1980.

6. H.C. Field, ed., *Dawn of Empire,* No. 2 of 96 parts, Netherlands, Time-Life Books, 1972.

7. *Purchas his Pilgrimes,* Vol. XIX, pp. 406-409.

# INDEX

132